Territorial Development in Latin America

This book explores one of the most pressing issues of our time: development, a concern that has persisted from the past century through to today, and is increasingly intertwined with challenges related to environmental sustainability and growing inequalities. Despite numerous academic and policy interventions, development remains an elusive goal. Hence, this book explains how conceptualisations of development, alternative to economic growth, have evolved in Latin American geographical literature and shows their practical applications in various contexts.

The book argues for a broader, more inclusive approach to development – territorial development – that integrates ecological, cultural, economic and social concerns. By focusing on territorial development seen from a theoretical perspective but also applied through case studies, the book underscores the importance of understanding the historical and power dynamics that influence how territories are shaped, for whom, and by whom. The book is divided into two parts. The first part provides a theoretical and historical background on development and territory in Latin America, presenting critical methodological perspectives for aligning academic research with community and environmental wellbeing. The second part consists of case studies that illustrate how different understandings of territory influence development agendas in diverse settings across the region.

Scholars, researchers and post-graduate students will find this an invaluable resource, as will policymakers and organisations interested in developmental practices.

Diana Morales is a Postdoctoral Researcher at the Centre for Innovation, Technology and Culture TIK, University of Oslo.

Laura Sariego-Kluge is a Lecturer and Researcher at the Escuela de Administración Pública, Universidad de Costa Rica, San José, Costa Rica.

Tiago Teixeira is a Senior Lecturer at Newcastle Business School, Northumbria University, Newcastle, UK.

RSA Regional Studies Association

A leading & impactful community

Routledge
Taylor & Francis Group

Regions and Cities

Series Editor in Chief
Joan Fitzgerald, *Northeastern University, USA*

Editors
Roberta Capello, *Politecnico di Milano, Italy*
Rob Kitchin, *Maynooth University, Ireland*
Jörg Knieling, *HafenCity University Hamburg, Germany*
Nichola Lowe, *University of Minnesota, USA*

In today's globalised, knowledge-driven and networked world, regions and cities have assumed heightened significance as the interconnected nodes of economic, social and cultural production, and as sites of new modes of economic and territorial governance and policy experimentation. This book series brings together incisive and critically engaged international and interdisciplinary research on this resurgence of regions and cities, and should be of interest to geographers, economists, sociologists, political scientists and cultural scholars, as well as to policy-makers involved in regional and urban development.

About the Regional Studies Association (RSA)

The RSA is the global community for regional and urban research, development and policy. As a learned society for regional studies, it provides an authoritative voice for researchers, students and practitioners from disciplines including economics, geography, political science, planning, urban sociology, transport planning and other fields. The RSA delivers its charitable aims through knowledge exchange and policy engagement activities, its portfolio of journals and publications, its programme of conferences and events and its worldwide territorial and research networks. The RSA also runs a grant funding programme and recognises good practice in regional studies through its awards. It is an inclusive, diverse and environmental responsible organisation. For more information go to www.regionalstudies.org

Territorial Development in Latin America

Cultural, Economic and Environmental Dimensions

Edited and translated by Diana Morales, Laura Sariego-Kluge and Tiago Teixeira

Routledge
Taylor & Francis Group
LONDON AND NEW YORK

Designed cover image: Getty Images / JarnoVerdonk

First published in English 2025
by Routledge
4 Park Square, Milton Park, Abingdon, Oxon OX14 4RN

and by Routledge
605 Third Avenue, New York, NY 10158

Routledge is an imprint of the Taylor & Francis Group, an informa business

British Library Cataloguing-in-Publication Data
A catalogue record for this book is available from the British Library

Library of Congress Cataloging-in-Publication Data
Names: Morales, Diana (Translator), editor. | Sariego-Kluge, Laura, editor. | Teixeira, Tiago, editor.
Title: Territorial development in Latin America : cultural, economic and environmental dimensions / edited and translated by Diana Morales, Laura Sariego-Kluge and Tiago Teixeira.
Other titles: Territorios y Desarrollo Desigual. English
Description: Abingdon, Oxon ; New York, NY : Routledge, 2025. | Series: Regions and cities | Includes bibliographical references and index.
Identifiers: LCCN 2024042159 (print) | LCCN 2024042160 (ebook) | ISBN 9781032650197 (hbk) | ISBN 9781032650227 (pbk) | ISBN 9781032650241 (ebk)
Subjects: LCSH: Economic development--Latin America.
Classification: LCC HC125 .T49813 2025 (print) | LCC HC125 (ebook) | DDC 338.98--dc23/eng/20250111
LC record available at https://lccn.loc.gov/2024042159
LC ebook record available at https://lccn.loc.gov/2024042160

ISBN: 978-1-032-65019-7 (hbk)
ISBN: 978-1-032-65022-7 (pbk)
ISBN: 978-1-032-65024-1 (ebk)

DOI: 10.4324/9781032650241

Typeset in Sabon
by SPi Technologies India Pvt Ltd (Straive)

This book is a translation of the Spanish original Morales, D.; Sariego-Kluge, L.; Teixeira, T. (eds.), 2022. Territorios y Desarrollo Desigual: Debates Actuales y Perspectivas Futuras desde una Óptica Latinoamericana. San José, Universidad de Costa Rica, CICAP ISBN 978-9968-932-44-8

Contents

Figures and Tables

Figures

Tables

Contributors

Ana Julia Cabrera Pacheco, PhD in Human Geography. Postdoctoral researcher El Colegio de la Frontera Sur and Postdoctoral Research Associate at the University of Edinburgh (Scotland).

Malena Castilla, PhD in Social Anthropology. Researcher at the National University of La Matanza and at the National Council of Scientific and Technical Research (Argentina).

Pamela Cichoski, PhD in Regional Development. Federal Technological University of Paraná, Brazil.

Maclovia Corrêa da Silva, PhD in Urban Environmental Structures. Professor at the Federal University of Technology – Paraná (Brazil).

Mariano Féliz, PhD in Social Sciences and PhD in Economics. Researcher at the Centre for Geographic Research of the Institute for Research in Humanities and Social Sciences (CIG-IdIHCS/CONICET-UNLP) (Argentina).

Ricardo Gomes Luiz, PhD and Researcher at the Federal University of Technology – Paraná (Brazil).

Diana Morales, PhD in Economic and Development Geographies. Researcher, University of Oslo.

Sebastián Saborío, PhD in Sociology. Professor and Researcher at the School of Sociology, University of Costa Rica.

Marcos Aurelio Saquet, PhD in Geography. Associate Professor, State University of the West of Paraná, Brazil.

Laura Sariego-Kluge, PhD in Economic Geography and Local Economic Development. Lecturer and Researcher, Universidad de Costa Rica.

Martín Nicolás Sotiru, Doctoral Fellow at the Centre for Geographic Research of the Institute for Research in Humanities and Social Sciences (CIG-IdIHCS/CONICET-UNLP) (Argentina).

Tiago Teixeira, PhD in Economic Geography. Senior Lecturer in International Business. Northumbria University.

Preface

This book, aimed at researchers, students, decision-makers, policymakers and practitioners interested in territorial development issues, reflects the complexity involved in thinking and constructing a notion of territory and development from the point of view of Latin American geography studies. In the chapters ahead, we intend to show the diversity of understandings and perspectives around the notions of territory and development in Latin American geography. In this literature, territories and their development are approached as dynamic spaces of power struggles, as spaces constituted by social, economic and cultural interaction with nature, and as spaces to exercise autonomy and rights.

The editors and translators have been working and discussing the contributions of Latin American authors on these topics since 2018, when we met at the Summer Institute in Economic Geography at the University of Gent. These efforts materialised in an online symposium, in the middle of the COVID-19 pandemic, that brought together Latin American researchers to present and discuss their work. The symposium, called 'Territories and Development in Latin America: Current Debates and Future Perspectives', which took place on February 4 and 5, 2021, had the support of the Centro de Investigación y Capacitación en Administración Pública (CICAP) and the Escuela de Administración Pública (EAP) of the Universidad de Costa Rica. During these discussions, a major conclusion was that Latin American researchers have reached great theoretical and empirical advances that can progress similar discussions occurring in other geographies and in fields such as geography and regional studies.

The symposium participants were invited to write a chapter for the book, emphasising on their contributions to build a wider analytical framework, which we attempt to summarise in Part 1. The book is divided into two parts. Part 1 explores the theoretical foundations and proposes a critical view of territories and development emerging from Latin American scholarship, as well as its differences and complementarities with Global North-based theorisations. Part 2 presents six case studies exploring empirically how territory is understood and what are the implications of such definitions on local and regional development.

Each chapter was evaluated by external academic peers, to whom we thank for their valuable contributions and time. We also thank the Universidad de Costa Rica for its support throughout the process, including Dr. Orlando Hernández, Director of CICAP; the administrative team of CICAP; the Director of the School of Public Administration, Angélica Vega, MSc; and the former director of EAP with whom we initiated the process, Dr. Leonardo Castellón. Finally, it is with great pleasure that we make this book available to the community interested in development and territorial issues in Latin America and beyond. Finally, we express our gratitude to the Regional Studies Association (RSA), for encouraging this translation exercise.

Dr. Diana Morales
Dr. Laura Sariego-Kluge
Dr. Tiago Teixeira
Editors and Translators

Part 1

Conceptual framework

1 Introduction

Diana Morales, Laura Sariego-Kluge and Tiago Teixeira

Development continues to be one of the most significant issues of our times; it has been a key concern of a multiplicity of disciplines and policy interventions. Yet, it remains an unfulfilled promise and so often comes back to academic and policy circles as an unsolved concern. Recent events such as the post-COVID-19 recovery, the volatility of interest rates, inflation, conflicts and wars, persistent poverty, and rising inequality, alongside grand challenges such as uneven development, climate change, and loss of biodiversity, expose the limitations of economistic approaches to development. Insofar as development theories continue to prioritise economic growth, the promises of wellbeing and progress for everyone, human and non-human, will remain unfulfilled. Under this premise, this book explores how various conceptualisations of territory and development are built and implemented across several regions in Latin America. The purpose is twofold: first, to evidence the contradictions and conflicts created by unidirectional views based on growth and modernisation; second, to show different ways of conceptualising and materialising alternative proposals.

To discuss development, it is also needed to discuss territory, as these two concepts are inextricably linked. There is a renewed interest to revisit territory across the Global North, since recent political narratives seem to claim territory as a space of state sovereignty, echoing former senses of imperial grandeur (Agnew, 2020). Furthermore, discussing and revisiting territory has been an ongoing task in Latin American geography; it may be time to put these sets of literature into conversation. Along the chapters, authors will show how territory is connected to the wellbeing of people and ecosystems. Territorial development, which is the concept we attempt to bring forward across the book, considers the history of power dynamics derived from colonialism and uneven participation in the global economy, the consequences of *by whom and for whom* territories are shaped and developed, and the value of popular and participatory knowledges. In this sense, the book shows alternatives for moving research beyond the inherent unevenness of capitalocentric views of development in territories. Defining territories and development is more than an academic task; it also has practical implications: such definitions influence local and regional development policies and rural and urban planning, as well as policies on land use or the creation of cooperation agreements between regions.

DOI: 10.4324/9781032650241-2

In Chapter 8, 'Building biocultural territories in the *Solares* of the Yucatán Peninsula, Mexico', Ana Julia Cabrera explains how traditional Mayan households in Mexico and their home gardens, *solares*, become *biocultural territories*. These familiar and intimate spaces are also spaces of resistance that ensure the subsistence of families, while integrating management of resources and coexistence between nature and culture.

In Chapter 9, 'Regional cooperation as local development agendas: Coffee Cultural Landscape (Colombia) and Coopeumo (Chile)', Diana Morales explains how regional cooperation strategies in Colombia and Chile respond to the socio-economic and cultural composition of the territories. The chapter dives into the influence of the territories (as a social construct) in the definition of regional cooperation agendas, which include how such processes influence local and regional development to try to solve problems caused by imposed, top-down economic policies.

In Chapter 10, 'Territorialisation of drug dealing in marginalised neighbourhoods of the Costa Rican capital', Sebastián Saborío examines territorial dynamics linked to drug dealing activities in Rincón Grande de Pavas, San José, Costa Rica. Challenging assumptions that illicit groups inherently establish territorial control, Saborío argues that drug dealers in this context engage in limited territorialisation—focused narrowly on securing drug sales rather than exerting broader dominance over the neighbourhood or its residents. While the impact on residents' daily lives is less severe than anticipated, these illicit activities still alter socio-spatial dynamics.

Finally, Chapter 11, 'Territories and development in Latin America', offers a series of conclusions and a reflective and critical perspective on how the volume contributes to wider debates and how to move forward with a research agenda. The book concludes with some reflections on the future direction of public policies on territorial development.

Bibliography

Agnew, J. (1994). The territorial trap: The geographical assumptions of international relations theory, *Review of International Political Economy*, 1(1), 53–80.

Agnew, J. (ed.) (2020). *The confines of territory*. Routledge.

Agnew, J. ed. (2023). *The confines of territory*. Routledge.

Amin, A. (1999). An institutionalist perspective on regional economic development, *International Journal of Urban and Regional Research*, 23(2), 365–378.

Amin, A. (2004). Regions unbound: Towards a new politics of place, *Geografiska Annaler, Series B: Human Geography*, 86(1), 33–44. https://doi.org/10.1111/j.0435-3684.2004.00152.x

Bezerra Carril, L. de F. (2006). Quilombo, territory and geography, *Agraria*, 3, 156–171.

Brenner, N. (2001). The limits to scale? Methodological reflections on scalar structuration, *Progress in Human Geography*, 25(4), 591–614. https://doi.org/10.1191/030913201682688959

Chatterton, P., and Gordon, N. (2004). *Taking back control: A journey through Argentina's popular uprising*. University of Leeds.
Dicken, P. (2007). *Global shift: Mapping the changing contours of the world economy*. 5th ed. New York: Guilford Press.
Ohmae, K. (1995). *The end of the nation state: The rise of regional economies*. Harper Collins.
Elden, S. (2013). *The birth of territory*. The University of Chicago Press.
Escobar, A. (1995). *Encountering development: The making and unmaking of the third world*. 2nd ed. Princeton University Press.
Haesbaert, R. (2013). From the myth of deterritorialization to multiterritoriality, *Culture and Social Representations*, 8(15), 9–42.
Haesbaert, R. (2019). Regional-global. Dilemmas of the region and regionalization in contemporary geography, *Locale*, 4(4), 169–174. https://doi.org/10.14409/rl.v4i4.9804
Halvorsen, S. (2019). Decolonising territory: Dialogues with Latin American knowledges and grassroots strategies, *Progress in Human Geography*, 43(5), 790–814. https://doi.org/10.1177/0309132518777623
Harvey, D. (2006). *The limits to capital*. London: Verso.
Larson, A.M., et al. (2016). The challenge of "Territory": Weaving the social fabric of indigenous communities in Nicaragua's Northern Caribbean autonomous region, *Bulletin of Latin American Research*, 35(3), 322–337. https://doi.org/10.1111/blar.12365
Lobao, L., Martin, R., and Rodríguez-Pose, A. (2009). Editorial: Rescaling the state: New modes of institutional-territorial organization, *Cambridge Journal of Regions, Economy and Society*, 2(1), 3–12. https://doi.org//10.1093/cjres/rsp001
Lopez Oropeza, M. (2010). Alternative models of local development from the periphery, *Eutopía - Territorial Economic Development Magazine*, (1). https://doi.org/10.17141/eutopia.1.2010.937
MacKinnon, D., and Cumbers, A. (2011). *Introduction to economic geography: Globalization uneven development and place*. 2nd ed. Pearson Prentice Hall.
Mançano, B. (2009). On the typology of territories, *Territórios e territorialidades: teorias, processesos e conflitos*, 197–215.
Martin, R., and Sunley, P. (1998). Slow convergence? The new endogenous growth theory and regional development, *Economic Geography*, 74(3), 201–227.
Massey, D. (1995). *Spatial divisions of labour: Social structures and the geography of production*. 2nd ed. Hampshire and London: Macmillan Press.
Painter, J. (2010). Rethinking territory, *Progress in Human Geography*, 42(5), 1090–1118.
Peck, J., Werner, M. and Jones, M. (2023). A dialogue on uneven development: a distinctly regional problem. *Regional Studies*, 57(7), 1392–1403.
Ruiz-Rivera, N., and Galicia, L. (2016). Geographic scale as an integrating concept in the understanding of socio-environmental problems, *Geographical Research*, 89, 137–153.
Saquet, M.A., and Sposito, E.S. (2009). *Territórios e territorialities: Theories, processes and conflicts, Geography in Questão*. Expressao Popular Editor. https://www.doi.org/10.48075/geoq.v13i3.21622
Scott, A.J., and Storper, M. (2007). Regions, globalization, development, *Regional Studies*, 41(1), 191–205.
Seval, M., Carné, M.A., Davies, C.L., and Fernández, V.R. (2020). A cluster policy in Argentina is also a breakthrough as a new development: Territorialization of experiences in pecan and dairy activities. *Networks*, 25(3), 1185–1211.

de Sousa Santos, B. (2016). Epistemologies of the south and the future, *From the European South*, 1, 17–29. http://europeansouth.postcolonialitalia.it
Svampa, M. (2015a). Commodities consensus: Neoextractivism and enclosure of the commons in Latin America, *South Atlantic Quarterly*, 114(1), 65–82. https://doi.org/10.1215/00382876-2831290
Svampa, M.N. (2015b). Southern feminisms and ecofeminisms, *New Society*, 256.
Swyngedouw, E. (1992). The Mammon Quest. "Glocalization", Interspatial Competition and the Monetary Order: The Construction of New Scales, in: M. Dunford and G. Kafkalas (Eds). *Cities and Regions in the New Europe*, Belhaven Press.

2 A brief history of development in Latin America

Laura Sariego-Kluge, Diana Morales and Tiago Teixeira

Introduction

Development became an academic and policy concern in the 1950s and has since been an object of multiple discussions, approximations, and experimentation. The discussions have predominated in fields such as economics, sociology, geography, and development studies, taking hold in Latin American geography until the end of the 1980s and the 1990s. In this chapter, we set out to explain the prominent approaches to development emerging from those debates. The first section addresses modernisation theory, dependency theory, and neoliberalism, top-down approaches that explain development from a macro-structural and normative paradigm. Seen critically, these approaches have ignored the diversity of Latin American territories, prompting struggles for political and economic power, forms of resistance, solidarity, and, consequently, the emergence of alternative forms of development. The second section explores the growing relevance of territorial development that emerged as a response to the region's colonial legacy and social injustices. The overall objective of this chapter is to provide an overview of the debates on development in Latin America and to set the context for Chapter 3, where we explore the main approaches to territory and territorial development in the region.

Modernisation and dependency theories

The Cold War, characterised by the intense rivalry between the United States and the former Soviet Union, had profound implications in Latin American countries. Amidst its agenda for geopolitical consolidation and efforts to counter the spread of communism, the United States sought to promote economic development and political stability in Latin America, and, therefore, align these countries with Western values and systems (Peet and Hartwick, 2015a,b). Consequently, development based on Western-model modernity became a priority in the national agendas of many Latin American nations (Willis, 2011). A theory that gained relevance during this period was the modernisation theory, which incorporated both economic and cultural dimensions to the notion of development. A classic example is Rostow's

DOI: 10.4324/9781032650241-3

(1960) model of historical stages of growth. Rostow argued that countries evolve progressively through five basic stages: 1) traditional society, characterised by subsistence agriculture; 2) productive, commercial, and export agriculture; 3) urbanisation, industrialisation, and technological progress; 4) maturity, that is, diversification of the industrial base; and 5) mass consumption, where industry surpasses the primary sector. According to the modernisation theory, underdevelopment was not merely an economic issue but also rooted in cultural differences. Hoselitz argued that the superior characteristics of the United States, Europe, and capitalist economic systems needed to be emulated for other countries to achieve progress (Bernstein, 1971). This could be achieved by replicating Western models of institutions, adopting a culture of consumption, and evolving from traditional social and cultural norms towards a capitalist economy based on rational and efficient economic decisions (Potter et al., 2008). Development was depicted as a linear, evolutionary process, underpinning a uniform, universalised, and binary (modern/traditional) vision, erasing any possibility for territorial diversity. Modernisation theorists were not especially concerned with spatial conceptualisations. However, it can be inferred that under such an approach territories are seen as containers of resources and factors of production (land, labour, and capital). The development of such territories depends on its inhabitants' abilities to organise, manage, and optimise the use of resources in modern ways and following capitalist interests.

In response to modernisation theory, scholars from the Global South developed a more critical perspective to explain *under*development. Dependency theory gained attention in the context of economic slowdown and crisis, between 1966 and 1980 (Larrain, 1989), to explain how the economic development of 'backward' nations was the result of the economic and political dominance of imperialism (Prebisch, 1950). For dependency theorists, European and North American development was contingent upon the underdevelopment of the 'rest', the periphery. The notions of centre and periphery emerged to explain the unequal relationships between countries, highlighting how such unequal exchanges favoured some countries to the detriment of others, since the periphery must satisfy the demands of the centre, limiting its development possibilities (Larrain, 1989). Not only was the centre–periphery relationship detrimental to creating development opportunities but, it is argued, creates an peripheral elite that would accumulate export profits for luxury consumption instead of internal investment, increasing inequality and masses of poor peasants (Prebisch, 1950; Kvangraven, 2021). To counteract these effects, development could be achieved by advancing national industries and markets. A classic example is the import-substitution economic strategy (Prebisch, 1950; Furtado, 2000). This policy, aimed at reducing a country's dependence on imported goods, includes promoting the production of those goods domestically and shielding domestic industries from foreign competition by introducing tariffs, quotas, and subsidies.

Despite falling out of the mainstream theorisations after the 1980s, currently, dependency theory remains influential in geographical research, especially in uneven development studies (Kvangraven, 2021). However, in relation to territory, dependency theory mostly considered the global and national scales, disregarding other important territorial dynamics. It offered a vision of territory as an object to create wealth from within, a mechanism for economic growth and development that results from exploiting endogenous assets.

Neoliberalism and development

While import-substitution policies did produce positive results in the industrialisation of some Latin American countries such as Brazil, state intervention also fostered the conditions for what is known as the 'Lost Decade' (Grinberg, 2022; Trovão and Dedecca, 2024; Valencia et al., 2023). By the 1980s, Latin American countries faced high levels of external debt and unemployment, hyperinflation, fiscal deficits, and overall economic stagnation (Dicken, 2011; Corbridge, 2008). In this context, neoliberalism, as an ideological and normative body of thought, started to shape the political agenda and development policies of Latin American countries. Under the leadership of the International Monetary Fund (IMF), the World Bank, and the United States Department of the Treasury, economic policy prescriptions were established in what is known as the Washington Consensus (Williamson, 1990). Those prescriptions were focused on achieving fiscal policy discipline, market-based interest rates, competitive exchange rates, reorienting public spending, implementing tax reforms, liberalising trade and foreign direct investment, privatising state enterprises, and deregulating and guaranteeing property rights (Stiglitz, 2002). These reforms were implemented throughout the region using several different tactics and interventions, even including violence, repression, and the installation of dictatorships (Taylor, 2002; Tinsman, 2004; Angeles-Castro 2021).

The adoption of neoliberalism in Latin American countries brought not only macro changes such as the opening to the international market. It also prompted decentralisation processes, increasing the power and responsibilities of subnational states and cities, including being responsible for their own development policies (Boisier, 1996). Decentralisation has opened spaces for social movements to claim a more prominent role in policymaking due to more direct contact with the centres of decision (Fernandes and de Jesus, 2021). In this context, scholars increasingly start to acknowledge the relevance of territories and their complex interplay with development. Therefore, one stream of literature and public policies influenced by Michael Storper's concept of the holy trinity and studies on the Marshallian industrial districts in Third Italy emerged to call attention to the relevance of endogenous resources for local development, and the ways in which subnational and local states could design their development policies (Brandâo, 2004). These studies explored the relevance of endogenous assets such as geographical proximity, local learning, local culture, cooperation, mutual trust and territorial identity, good governance, and social capital in fostering competitive advantages, and, consequently, endogenous development (Fernandes and de Jesus, 2021; Pecqueur, 2009; Méndez, 2002). However, territorial power relations and existing uneven outcomes are overlooked in such studies, given that they emphasise on how firm and non-firm actors work collectively around common interests to foster development.

All these political and economic reforms were supposed to finally bring development to Latin American countries. However, the promises of development and poverty reduction did not materialise, and social inequality increased (Harvey, 2005; Angeles-Castro, 2021). A critical view of neoliberal economic policies explains how these have increased social inequalities by commodifying and privatising land, resulting in the dispossession of peasants, suppressing rights to the commons, commodifying the labour force, erasing alternative forms of production and consumption, and driving the appropriation of natural resources (Perreault and Martin, 2005; Harvey, 2005; Berndt, Werner and Fernández, 2020). Under neoliberalism, still the dominant approach to development in Latin America, regions and territories are considered successful if they can harness the potential of the global economy, without considering how local institutions incorporate and adapt neoliberalism to their realities (Birch and Siemiatycki, 2016). In neoliberalism, territories are spaces regulated under market relations, supply and demand, pricing mechanisms, market efficiency, and competition, a place to attract private companies and foreign direct investment.

The Pink Tide and neoextractivism

Neoliberal policies generated numerous pockets of resistance in Latin America, giving rise to another important shift in development policies. The so-called Pink Tide during the early 2000s, a political wave that swept across the region, saw the rise of left-leaning governments in countries such as Venezuela, Bolivia, Ecuador, Argentina, and Brazil. These administrations, characterised by their progressive social policies and opposition to neoliberal economic models, sought to redefine development paradigms by focusing on social inclusion, poverty reduction, and wealth redistribution. These reforms also came accompanied by the institutionalisation of development alternatives, for example, the enactment of the rights of nature in the Ecuadorian Constitution, or the declaration of the Bolivian State as a multi-ethnic and multicultural nation (Escobar, 2015; Svampa, 2019; Sánchez and Polga-Hecimovich, 2019).

The Pink Tide was accompanied by a commodities boom and a series of social reforms that partly addressed inequalities and acknowledged cultural diversity (Fishwick and Selwyn, 2016; Kingstone, 2018). A key element of its development model was the assertion of state control over natural resources and the promotion of what academia has called neoextractivism—an economic strategy that emphasises large-scale extraction of natural resources such as oil, gas, and minerals to generate revenue for social programmes, with significant state involvement and control over these resources (Svampa 2015, 2019). This approach was seen as a means to leverage the region's abundant natural resources to fund social welfare initiatives and infrastructure development, thereby reducing inequality and fostering economic growth.

This neoextractivist model has been subject to significant criticism and debate. Not only has it done little to change the role of Latin American economies as providers of raw materials for the global markets. It also has perpetuated dependency on commodity exports, intensified environmental degradation, social conflicts, and the marginalisation of indigenous and Afro-Latinos communities (Merino, 2020; Marston, 2022). Even though new political narratives emerging from social movements, such as Buen Vivir and the Rights of Nature, challenge the traditional development models and propose alternative ways of relating to the environment and economic development, it is also argued that these alternatives were limited from their very formulation (Svampa, 2019; Merino, 2020).

Despite the large differences between the dominant approaches to development, we observe that these continue to prioritise national scales, employ top-down decision-making processes, and treat territories as economic assets that should be exploited to serve broader economic agendas.

Territorial development

Another stream of literature, which this book is interested in, is Latin American decolonial studies, where the concepts of territory and territorial development gained relevance since the 1990s. Such studies were spurred by the organisation and political resurgence of social movements and other civil society entities (Schneider, 2010). According to Saquet (2018), these studies proposed a revaluation of the traditional positivist approaches to territory as a physical space (often a demarcated space under state power), incorporating new decolonial theories and methodologies. Territory is conceptualised based on three main characteristics. First, territories are appropriated and dominated and, therefore, reflect power relations and control manifested around cultural, political, economic, and environmental dynamics. Second, territories are constructed through various scales (global to local). Third, territories are historically constructed through expressions of power relations at a given historical moment (Saquet, 2018). Such literature takes into consideration different dimensions of power relations such as political (state power at multiple scales, but also considers non-state actors), cultural (symbolic appropriation by a group of actors and their territorial identity), and economic (marked by economic relations) (Fuini, 2014).

This shift in how territories were viewed, understood, and acted upon was relevant as it has substantial implications for Latin American debates on what has been termed 'territorial development' (Saquet, 2007). Territorial development proposes a multifaceted approach that prioritises the importance of local contexts in shaping development policies and practices (Dallabrida et al., 2021). These studies focus on the places where people live, feel, interact, and experience social, political, cultural, economic, and natural relationships, including subaltern struggles and resistances against exploitation and claiming better living conditions (Saquet, 2007, 2018; Schneider, 2010). This literature also highlights the voices of marginalised communities, such as indigenous groups, placing attention on their knowledge and bringing into light historical injustices and resistances. It also emphasises on the need to integrate cultural heritage into development strategies, promoting community-driven sustainable practices and initiatives, and fostering social cohesion, community participation and empowerment (Saquet, 2018). Existing studies on territorial approaches to development will be explored in-depth in Chapters 3 and 4, as well as in the case studies in Part 2.

Conclusions

In this chapter, we have explored the debates on development with the largest influence in Latin America. As discussed, three main theories and approaches to development have been dominant since the second half of the 20th century: modernisation theory, dependency theory, and neoliberalism, followed by more recent ideas on neoextractivism. Additionally, we have introduced how Latin American geographers have conceptualised territorial development, and its overall relevance for development practices and policies, which takes into consideration local communities and their realities.

Proponents of the modernisation theory claimed that development was a linear and evolutionary process; therefore, Latin American countries would go through several stages until achieving modernisation. Modernisation theory scholars argued that for Latin American countries to reach development, there was a need for a cultural shift to allow replicating Western models of institutions, social and cultural norms based on rationality, and a capitalist economy guided by efficient economic decisions (Potter et al., 2008). On the other hand, dependency theory emerged as a critical response, looking to explain underdevelopment as a consequence of unequal trade relationships between the centre and periphery (the Global North and the Global South). Dependency theorists argue that underdevelopment results because of unequal exchanges in the global market, where the periphery sells raw materials to be transformed in the centre, to then buy them again at higher prices. Such a theory influenced many Latin American countries to adopt import-substitution model and a developmental form of state mostly based on top-down decisions.

However, as shown, both theories were problematic. On the one hand, modernisation theory approached territories as containers of resources and factors of production, and development as a uniform, evolutionary, and universalised process, which downplayed territorial diversity. On the other hand, dependency theory paid attention to the global and national scales, overlooking internal territorial dynamics. Territory becomes a means of exploitation to generate internal wealth, and development is steered narrowly based on national top-down decisions.

The shift to neoliberalism since the 1980s brought another transformative phase in Latin America. Neoliberalism has and continues to influence Latin American countries' approaches to development. Under this context, most Latin American countries conceived development mainly in economic terms of market deregulation, international trade, fiscal discipline, and privatisation. Neoliberalism also accelerated decentralisation, making territories responsible for fostering their own success (e.g., by attracting foreign direct investment).

The adoption of neoliberalism in Latin America had serious consequences in social inequality, and the region has seen an increase in socioeconomic and environmental conflict and power disputes. Under this context, Latin American studies on territory and territorial development—within human and economic geography—began to emerge to explain such conflicts and power disputes. This has resulted in a substantial ontological and epistemological renovation in Latin American geography and in development studies (Haesbaert, 2018). In such studies, the concept of territory gained centrality: territories are approached and examined as marked and shaped by power dynamics related to different dimensions of social relations, such as cultural, political, economic, and environmental. Additionally, territories are seen as constructed through various scales, from global to local, and as a historical process, which reflects dominant power relations at specific moments (Saquet, 2018).

This growing relevance of territorial development research in Latin America since the 1990s represents a challenge to Eurocentric approaches and a crucial shift towards a more inclusive and context-sensitive approach to development, therefore, with potential implications for development policies in Latin America. This approach emphasises local contexts and experiences in shaping development practices (Dallabrida et al., 2021), highlighting the value of marginalised communities such as indigenous groups and their knowledge/cultural heritage, the need to address historical injustices and encourage resistance and change, the promotion of community-driven sustainable practices, and fostering social cohesion through community participation and empowerment (Saquet, 2018). Overall, the understanding of territories as dynamic and complex spaces marked by power dynamics at multiple scales and dimensions provides a nuanced and inclusive framework for understanding and promoting development in Latin America.

In conclusion, this chapter has sought to provide a general discussion and contextualisation of key Latin American debates on development, including the relevance of territorial development studies. Chapter 3 will examine in-depth mainstream territorial approaches in Latin America and provide a more detailed account of what such approaches entail and consist of.

Bibliography

Angeles-Castro, G. (2021). *Economic Liberalization in Latin America. Routledge Studies in Development Economics*. London and New York: Routledge.

Berndt, C., Werner, M., and Fernández, V.R. (2020). Postneoliberalism as institutional recalibration: Reading Polanyi through Argentina's soy boom, *Environment and Planning A: Economy and Space*, 52(1), 216–236.

Bernstein, H. (1971). Modernisation theory and the sociological study of development, *The Journal of Development Studies*, 7(2), 141–160. https://doi.org/10.1080/00220387108421356

Birch, K., and Siemiatycki, M. (2016). Neoliberalism and the geographies of marketization: The entangling of state and markets, *Progress in Human Geography*, 40(2), 177–198.

Boisier, S. (1996). Em busca do esquivo desenvolvimento regional: entre a caixa-preta e o projeto político, *Planejamento e políticas públicas*, 13, 1–33.

Brandâo, C. (2004). Teorias, estratégias e políticas regionais e urbanas recentes: anotações para uma agenda do desenvolvimento territorializado. *Revista Paranaense de Desenvolvimento*, (107), 57–76.

Corbridge, S. (2008). The (im)possibility of development studies, *Economy and Society*, 37(1), 175–191.

Dallabrida, V.R., Rotta, E., Büttenbender, P.L., Denardin, V.F., and Arenhart, L.O. (2021). Territorial approach of development: Conceptual categories and methodological assumptions, *Revista Brasileira de Desenvolvimento Territorial Sustentável*, 7(1).

Dicken, P. (2011). *Global shift: Mapping the changing contours of the world economy*. SAGE Publications.

Escobar, A. (2015). Territorios de diferencia: la ontología política de los "derechos al territorio", *Cuadernos de antropología social*, (41), 25–38.

Fernandes, V.R.V., and de Jesus, C.M. (2021). Síntese Teórica para a Análise do Desenvolvimento Territorial, *Revista Estudo & Debate*, 28(4), https://doi.org/10.22410/issn.1983-036X.v28i4a2021.2782

Fishwick, A., and Selwyn, B. (2016). Labour-centred development in Latin America: Two cases of alternative development, *Geoforum*, 74, 233–243.

Fuini, L.L. (2014). Território e geografia no Brasil: uma revisão bibliográfica, *Formação* (Online), 1(21).

Furtado, C. (2000). *Teoria política do desenvolvimento econômico*. São Paulo: Paz e Terra.

Grinberg, N. (2022). The political economy of the 'Lost Decade', *Review of International Political Economy*, 29(1), 100–126.

Haesbaert, R. (2018). De categoria de análise a categoria da prática: a multiplicidade do territorio numa perspectiva latino-americana. In: F. Fridman, L.A. Gennari and S. Lencioni (Eds.), *Políticas públicas e territorios: onze estudos latino-americanos*, pp. 267–288. CLACSO.

Harvey, D. (2005). *Spaces of neoliberalization: Towards a theory of uneven geographical development*, Vol. 8. Franz Steiner Verlag.

Kingstone, P. (2018). *The political economy of Latin America: Reflections on neoliberalism and development after the commodity boom*. Second ed. Routledge.

Kvangraven, I.H. (2021). Beyond the stereotype: Restating the relevance of the dependency research programme, *Development and Change*, 52(1), 76–112.

Larrain, J. (1989). *Theories of development: Capitalism, colonialism and dependency*. Cambridge: Polity Press.

Marston, A. (2022). *Extractivist states: Contesting and negotiating the "Commodities Consensus" in Bolivia, Ecuador, and Across Latin America*, pp. 194–200.

Méndez, R. (2002). Innovación y desarrollo territorial: algunos debates teóricos recientes, *Eure* (Santiago), 28(84), 63–83.

Merino, R. (2020). The cynical state: Forging extractivism, neoliberalism and development in governmental spaces, *Third World Quarterly*, 41(1), 58–76.

Pecqueur, B. (2009). A guinada territorial da economia global, *Política & Sociedade*, 8(14), 79–106.

Peet, R., and Hartwick, E. (2015a). *Theories of development: Contentions, arguments, alternatives*. Guilford Publications.

Peet, R. and Hartwick, E. (2015b). *Theories of development: Contentions, arguments, alternatives*. Third edition. New York and London: Guilford Publications.

Perreault, T., and Martin, P. (2005). Geographies of neoliberalism in Latin America, *Environment and Planning A*, 37(2), 191–201.

Potter, R.B., et al. (2008). *Geographies of development: An introduction to development studies*. Pearson Education.

Prebisch, R. (1950). *Crecimiento, desequilibrio y disparidades: interpretación del proceso de desarrollo económico*. Santiago, Chile: Estudio Económico de América Latina 1949, Economic Commission for Latin America and the Caribbean (ECLAC).

Rostow, W. (1960). *The stages of economic growth: A non-communist manifesto*. First edition. Cambridge: Cambridge University Press.

Sánchez, F., and Polga-Hecimovich, J. (2019). The tools of institutional change under post-neoliberalism: Rafael Correa's Ecuador, *Journal of Latin American Studies*, 51(2), 379–408.

Saquet, M. (2007). *Abordagens e concepções de território*. São Paulo: Expressão Popular.

Saquet, M.A. (2018). A descoberta do território e outras premissas do desenvolvimento territorial, *Revista Brasileira de Estudos Urbanos e Regionais*, 20, 479–505.

Schneider, S. (2010). Análisis multidimensional y escalar del desarrollo territorial en Brasil, *Eutopía: Revista de Desarrollo Económico Territorial*, (1), 25–49. https://doi.org/10.17141/eutopia.1.2010.765

Stiglitz, J.E. (2002). *Globalization and its discontents*. New York and London: Norton.

Svampa, M. (2015). Commodities consensus: Neoextractivism and enclosure of the commons in Latin America. *South Atlantic Quarterly*, 114(1), 65–82.

Svampa, M. (2019). *Neo-extractivism in Latin America: Socio-environmental conflicts, the territorial turn, and new political narratives*. Cambridge University Press.

Taylor, M. (2002). Success for whom? An historical-materialist critique of neoliberal Chile, *Historical Materialism*, 10(2), 45–75.

Tinsman, H. (2004). More than victims: Women agricultural workers and social change in rural Chile. in P. Winn (Ed.), *Victims of the Chilean miracle: Workers and neoliberalism in the Pinochet era 1972–2002*. Durham: Duke University Press.

Trovão, C. J. B.M., and Dedecca, C.S. (2024). The 2010s in Brazil: A lost decade in the dimensions of production, productivity and labor, *Economia e Sociedade*, 33, 123–147.

Valencia, Á.D.V., Oliva, L.E.M., and Montiel, A.G.C. (2023). Economic growth and its components in South America: Performance in the period 1950–2019, *Revista de ciencias sociales*, 29(3), 26–40.

Williamson, J. (1990). *Latin American adjustment: How much has happened?*, Vol. 4. Washington, DC: Institute for International Economics.

Willis, K. (2011). *Theories and practices of development*. Routledge.

3 Territory and development in regional studies and Latin American literature

Diana Morales, Laura Sariego-Kluge and Tiago Teixeira

Introduction

As shown in Chapter 2, development has often been equated to economic growth, becoming the goal of territorial transformations and the focus of theories of development, dominant literature, and public policy up until today (Gudynas, 2017; J. T. Murphy, 2008; Rosenman et al., 2020). Limiting development to economic growth has meant that key geographical concepts, such as territory, have been narrowed down to spaces to create and retain growth. This book shows how that vision limits how researchers can produce insights and promote transformative change.

Approaching territories critically is a conversation with an important tradition in Latin American Geography (Haesbaert, 2019), and slowly extending across the Global North (e.g., Painter, 2010; Halvorsen, 2019; Morales et al., 2024). However, before entering to explain the contributions of Latin American critical geography to rethinking territories as a spatial concept, we offer an overview of territories in Anglo-Saxon economic geography and regional studies. This will be followed by some reflections on how the conceptualisation of territory has evolved and the potential of its analytical power.

Territory in Anglo-Saxon economic geography and regional studies

Economic geography and regional studies research have been concerned with understanding the economic processes transforming the space. Research has shown how territories are created, shaped, and transformed by socio-economic phenomena, making space a fundamental element to explain economic activities (Sheppard et al. 2012; MacKinnon & Cumbers, 2018). Economic geography has amply discussed spatial concepts such as regions and territories, as well as their transformation within the globalised economy (Painter, 2010). However, being economic geography traditionally developed and inspired by the economic development of the Global North (Pollard et al., 2009), the conceptualisation of territory has a Global North bias and an emphasis on economic constructions (Morales et al., 2024).

DOI: 10.4324/9781032650241-4

Territory as a concept has evolved to explain how space transforms and is transformed due to the materialisation of economic relations. Earlier literature approached territory as the space for the development of capitalist economies (Agnew, 1994). There was a focus on strategies with a strong spatial component, such as industrial districts, agglomerative economies, and clusters (Storper, 1997), looking to explain regional economic prosperity. This approximation acknowledges that the territories are defined by economic processes and not only by the jurisdictional borders where the state exercises its power. Yet, it remains limited by not recognising that territories are dynamic spaces that evolve and are transformed by processes beyond a capitalist economy.

Acknowledging the dynamic nature of territories came with the advance of economic globalisation. During the 1990s, territory was explained in relation to the changes it was experiencing due to economic globalisation and the decentralisation of state power (Agnew, 1994). Thus, the debates advanced towards explaining the multiscalar networks connecting regions with the global economy (Amin, 2004). Theories of scale and rescaling associated with economic globalisation and away from Fordism emerged, bringing the debates about the hollowing out of the state (Jessop, 2013). Literature focused on explaining how states began to lose control of exchange rates, foreign investment, employment, and the relocation of companies. Accordingly, the state began to lose power in the economy and was replaced by financial institutions and global markets without territorial roots (Martin & Sunley, 1998; Ōmae & Ohmae, 1995). It was argued that the proliferation of transnational integration and multinational companies, plus the extraterritorial nature of capital and information, made the national scale almost redundant (Ōmae & Ohmae, 1995). Territories became glocalised spaces for economic competition, while demanding greater autonomy and the decentralisation of powers from the national state (Swyngedouw, 1992).

Economic globalisation has deeply transformed territories and regions (Dicken, 2007). Increased competition between regions, agglomeration policies, regional innovation systems, local and regional development, and urbanisation began to dominate local and regional development agendas and shape local economic geographies (Scott and Storper, 2007). Thus, in Anglo-Saxon literature, territory goes from being understood as a space for the exercise of sovereign power to a space for economic development and globalisation. The conceptual evolution of the concept of territory is influenced by the economic transition from a Fordist to a globalised era with emphasis on technological progress, modernisation, and agglomeration. This approach places regions as spaces for the materialisation of the global economy.

Evolution of territory in Latin American geography

Traditionally, territory has been conceptualised in relation to its capacity to contain public policies and jurisdictional borders. Territory is a unit where laws and public policies are applied, that is, a government space subdivided into countries, provinces, departments, and municipalities, among others (Mançano, 2009). It is with this vision that economic development policies have been designed and applied.

Latin American literature refers to this conceptualisation of territory as a normative concept. Accordingly, the normative model gathers perspectives on how territory and its development should be understood, based on the point of view of policymakers, social groups, and academia. Therefore, it is argued, territorial development is achieved through planning, neoliberalising the economy, decentralising state powers, and empowering communities to foster social change to harness the benefits of a market economy (López Sandoval et al., 2017; Haesbaert, 2020). An illustration of this approach can be found in countries highly dependent on the extraction of raw materials. In these cases, the state promotes development via international and private investment and manage the imbalances between the centre and the periphery by redistributing the wealth created by the export of raw materials (Gudynas, 2009; López Sandoval et al., 2017).

The normative perspective of territory is enhanced by supranational organisations such as the Inter-American Development Bank (IDB), the United Nations Economic Commission for Latin America and the Caribbean (ECLAC), and the World Bank, which promote territory as a subnational spatial unit for state intervention. Accordingly, political-administrative functions can be delegated to reduce the size of the state, increasing efficiency and saving resources (Boisier, 2004; Manzanal, 2007; Bervejillo, 1995). This approach, it is argued, facilitates attaining the economic opportunities offered by globalisation, and implementing strategies based on endogenous development, therefore increasing the socio-economic importance of territories for countries (Vázquez Barquero and Rodríguez Cohard, 2019). Under these premises, decentralisation allows involving different actors at local and regional scales, and the recognition of local values and demands to foster economic development, rather than following top-down mandates from the capital.

With the consolidation of the geography of territories as a field of study (Haesbaert 2020; López Sandoval et al., 2017), the normative vision of territory has expanded to highlight the importance of redistributing resources and designing territorial development policies based on social justice criteria (Braudel, 1985; Santos, 1996; Harvey, 2004). From this perspective, territorial development is a necessary condition for the exercise of citizenship, for guaranteeing basic rights, and for promoting the welfare of the population. To achieve these goals, it is essential to recognise territorial diversity and create greater cohesion between the different regions in a country, especially between the centres and the peripheries. This would imply recognising and legitimising the existence of territorial diversity and the demands of local populations to model their own development modes (Haesbaert, 2006; 2014).

As a normative concept, territory is deeply linked to sovereign power and territory as an economic space, at least from the point of view of public policies and theory of the state. However, this vision can contribute to conflict and confrontations. The United Nations Economic Commission for Latin America and the Caribbean reported that between 2015 and 2019, there were at least 1,223 conflicts in 13 countries as a result of transgressions on indigenous territories related to interests of extractive industries such as mining, hydrocarbons, energy, and monocultures (Maldonado Valera et al., 2021). These conflicts often occur due to a confrontation between different visions of territory and territorial development. Indeed, some of the main conflicts stem from a confrontation with a vision of territory based on extractivist capitalism and processes of wealth accumulation versus a vision of territories as spaces for life. This vision often responds to interests coming from above, national or international firms, governments, and international public bodies; or from below, from criminal groups that appropriate, delimit, and define territories outside the law for their own advantages (Bezares, 2018). The confluence of these groups and interests can affect the configuration of territories in such a way that multi-territorialities emerge in the contention for dominating space (Haesbaert, 2013). Another source of conflicts over territory is the neoliberal vision that categorises some territories as 'unproductive' or 'inadequate' for capital expansion, conflicting with communities that have different appreciations of their land and ways of inhabiting it. These conflicts include disputes over urban planning and the inclusion of protected areas (Barbosa, 2021; Cabrera, 2022).

As a response and inspired by the work of activists' collectives and social movements (Camargo & Ojeda, 2017; Quimbayo Ruiz, 2020), critical Latin American authors propose an approach to territory as a space for the dispute of power, for the exercise of a diversity of development agendas, and a combination of identities, cultures, and political processes (Rogério Haesbaert, 2013; Mançano, 2009; Saquet & Sposito, 2009). This definition is broader; it focuses on power relations and recognises that the territory is defined, inhabited, and disputed by a diversity of actors, social groups, and institutions that are not only diverse among themselves but have their own agendas. This approach recognises that power is exercised by all actors, even if unevenly, showing that power is also an exercise of resistance (Haesbaert, 2013). These relationships are not only constituted between social groups and individuals among themselves but are also exercised in relation to the non-human and the natural world (Escobar, 1995; Svampa, 2015).

Territory as a space of power dispute and conflict is, perhaps, one of the most valuable contributions of Latin American geographical literature. However, some authors have pointed out how linking territory and power can set attention away from other social and cultural processes that also shape territories (Saquet and Sposito, 2009), namely, territory as an exercise of autonomy that emerges within the framework of social and class struggles (Bezerra Carril, 2005; Gordon & Chatterton, 2004). Further, from the perspective of indigenous and ancestral peoples, territory is also understood as a space for cultural preservation and the exercise of autonomy and rights, demanding the recognition of multiple ways of living and inhabiting the space (Larson et al., 2016) (Chapter 8 will explain this point in more detail).

Finally, another key contribution of Latin American geography is Territories as Practice. Practice refers to the socio-material and socio-spatial actions carried out by communities and social groups to perform their ways of life, self-recognition, and empowerment (Haesbaert, 2020). In Latin American geography, these ideas have been used to explain how communities, through their everyday actions and language, resist development and capitalism (Gutiérrez Aguilar, 2014). Territories as practice in geographical research has been mostly developed by the work of Rogelio Haesbaert (2018, 2019, 2020). Accordingly, territories as practice refers to the common use of the word by most social groups, the everyday understanding of the territory related to their knowledge and lives. Therefore, territories as practice includes a range of socio-material and socio-spatial actions, from the ancestral practices of native communities to actions of resistance to economic and political domination, and everyday socio-economic activities such as practices of production, consumption and disposal (Morales et al., 2024). Territories are also spaces for the reproduction of life, ecosystems of cultural, economic, natural, political, and geographical dimensions developed and cared for by communities with their own organisational structures, worldviews, and values sustained over time (Barbosa, 2021).

Conclusions

In a context where development promises have not been delivered and regional inequality continues to rise across the world, a deeper and critical view of key geographical concepts can help to better engage and inform debates, theory, and practice. '[A] Latin American perspective on territory is characterized by plurality, involving a multiplicity of social subjects' (Haesbaert, 2020, p. 147). Latin American literature has broadened the understanding of territory by studying social struggles and demands for territory and autonomy throughout the region since colonial times. Accordingly, territory, as a geographical concept, pays special attention to the conflicts generated by development models that are considered exclusionary, colonial, and homogenising (Svampa, 2015).

As the case studies in this book will show, policies and interventions focused on economic growth tend to generalise and homogenise development and underdevelopment, but the practice, understanding, and translation of these policies evidence the conflicts, contradictions, and trade-offs. These conflicts and contradictions are part of the conceptualisation of territory, and its acknowledgement may be a key step in proposing locally sensitive solutions. In this sense, territory can be considered an arena of dispute where local actors confront global and national forces, often requiring interventions at multiple scales for territorial autonomy to be recognised (López Sandoval et al., 2017; Haesbaert, 2020).

Different perspectives coexist, from a vision that conceives territory as a container of natural resources and economic interests to others that see it as a dynamic space shaped by social relations and local agency. The conflicts over territory reflect these divergent views, whether they arise from struggles over land control or from tensions between different actors regarding the direction of territorial development. Moving forward, it is crucial to recognise the complexity of territories, the diversity of interests at play, and the need for inclusive governance mechanisms that allow for the negotiation of these differences and the pursuit of more equitable and sustainable forms of territorial development.

Bibliography

Agnew, J. (1994). The territorial trap: The geographical assumptions of international relations theory. *Review of International Political Economy*, 1(1), 53–80.

Amin, A. (2004). Regions unbound: towards a new politics of place. *Geografiska Annaler: Series B, Human Geography*, 86(1), 33–44. Available at: https://doi.org/10.1111/j.0435-3684.2004.00152.x

Andrade, M. (1998). Territorialidades, desterritorialidades, nuevas territorialidades: os limites do poder nacional e do poder local. En: M. Santos, M. Souza, and M. Silveira (Orgs.). *Territorio, globalización y fragmentación*, pp. 213–220. Hucitec.

Arendt, H. (1969). *On violence*. Harcourt, Brace and World.

Barbosa, L. (2021). De las mujeres como energía vital y las reverberaciones de la lucha en defensa de los territorios y de los comunes en América Latina. En: A. Calderón Cisneros, M. Olivera Bustamante, and M. Arellano Nucamendi (eds.), *Territorios para la vida. Mujeres en defensa de sus bienes naturales y por la sostenibilidad de la vida* (pp. 23–55). UNICACH.

Bazzo, W.A., Linsingen, I.V., and Pereira, L.T. do V. (2003). *Introdução aos estudos CTS (Ciência, Tecnologia e Sociedade)*. Organização dos Estados Ibero-americanos para a Educação, a Ciência e a Cultura (OEI). http://oei.es/salactsi/Livro_CTS_OEI.pdf

Bervejillo, F. (1995). Territorios en la globalización: nuevos procesos y estrategias de desarrollo. *Prisma*, 25 (4), 9–52.

Bezares, H. (2018). Governing the Mexican drug war: a political geography of public security and the organisation of everyday violence. Doctoral Thesis. University of Newcastle, UK. http://hdl.handle.net/10443/4164

Bezerra Carril, L.F. (2005). Quilombo, território e geografia. *Agrária (São PauloOnline)*, 3, 156–171.

Boisier, S., 2004. *Desarrollo endógeno:¿ para qué?,¿ para quién*. El humanismo en una interpretación contemporánea del desarrollo. Available at www.ponencia-boisiercedetuar.pdf

Braudel, F. (1985). *La dynamique du capitalisme*. Les Editions Arthaud.

Bridgewater, P., and Rotherham, I. (2019). Una perspectiva crítica sobre el concepto de diversidad biocultural y su papel emergente en la conservación de la naturaleza y el patrimonio. *Gente Nat.* 1, 291– 304. https://doi.org/10.1002/pan3.10040

Brown, J., Flint, T., and LaMay, J. (2020, May 1). The politics of pineapple: Examining the inequitable impacts of Southern Costa Rica's pineapple industry. *Journal of Public & International Affairs*. https://jpia.princeton.edu/news/politics-pineapple-examining-inequitable-impacts-southern-costa-ricas-pineapple-industry

Cabrera, A.J. (2022). Construyendo territorios bioculturales desde el solar familiar en la Península de Yucatán, México. In: D. Morales, L. Sariego, and T. Teixeira (eds.), *Territorios y desarrollo: Teorías, debates y casos desde América Latina*. San José: CICAP, Universidad de Costa Rica.

Camargo, A. and Ojeda, D. (2017). Ambivalent desires: State formation and dispossession in the face of climate crisis. *Political Geography*, 60, 57–65.
Cara, R.B. (1998). Territorialidade e identidade regional no Sul da Província de Buenos Aires. En: M. Santos, M. Souza and M. Silveira (Orgs.). *Territorio, globalización y fragmentación*, 261–269. Hucitec.
Cruz, M. (2018). Cosmovisión andina e interculturalidad: Una mirada al desarrollo sostenible desde el *sumak kawsay*. *Revista Chakiñán de Ciencias Sociales y Humanidades*, (5), 119–132. http://scielo.senescyt.gob.ec/scielo.php?script=sci_arttext&pid=S2550-67222018000100119&lng=es&tlng=es
de Souza, M.L. (1996). A teorização sobre o desenvolvimento em uma época de fadiga teórica, ou: sobre a necessidade de uma "teoria aberta" do desenvolvimento sócio-espacial. *Territorio, Laget/UFRJ*, 1(1), 5–22.
Días, R. (2011). O que é a política científica y tecnológica? *Sociologías*, *13*(28), 316–344. https://doi.org/10.1590/S1517-45222011000300011
Dicken, P. (2007). *Global shift: Mapping the changing contours of the world economy*. Fifth ed. Sage Publications.
Escobar, A. (1995). *Encountering Development: The Making and Unmaking of the Third World*. Princeton: Princeton University Press.
Escobar, A. (2005). El "postdesarrollo" como concepto y práctica social. En: Mato, D. (coord.). *Políticas de economía, ambiente y sociedad en tiempos de globalización*. Universidad Central de Venezuela.
Escolar, M. (1993). Territórios de dominação estatal e fronteiras nacionais: a mediação geográfica da representação e da sobrenia política. En: M. Santos, M.A. de Souza, F.C. Scarlato and M. Arroyo (eds.). *O novo mapa do mundo: Fim de Século e Globalização*, pp. 27–52. Hucitec.
Fals Borda, O. (2000). *Acción y espacio: autonomías en la nueve República*. IEPRI.
FAO. (2018). Pesticides use. Global, regional and country trends, 1990–2018. *FAOSTAT Analytical Brief* 16. Food and Agriculture Organization of the United Nations. https://www.fao.org/3/cb3411en/cb3411en.pdf
Fernández, B. (2008). Sobre una tipología de territorios. En: M. Saquet and E. Savério (eds.). *Territórios e territorialidades: teorias, processos e conflitos*. Expresão Popular: UNESP.
Frank, A. (1967). *Capitalismo y subdesarrollo en América Latina*. Siglo XXI.
Gordon, N. and Chatterton, P. (2004). *Taking back control: a journey through Argentina's popular uprising*. Leeds: School of Geography, University of Leeds.
Gudynas, E. (2009). Diez Tesis Urgentes sobre el Nuevo Extractivismo: Contextos y Demandas Bajo el Progresismo Sudamericano Actual. In: J. Schuldt, A. Acosta, A. Barandiará, A. Bebbington, M. Folchi, CEDLA–Bolivia, A. Alayza and E. Gudynas (eds.). *Extractivismo, Política y Sociedad*, pp. 187–225. CAAP/CLAES.
Gudynas, E. (2017). Post-development and other critiques of the roots of development. In: *The essential guide to critical development studies* (pp. 84–93). Routledge.
Gutiérrez Aguilar, R. (2014). *Rhythms of the Pachakuti: Indigenous uprising and state power in Bolivia*. Duke University Press.
Haesbaert, R. (2006). Ordenamento territorial. *Boletim goiano de Geografia*, 26(1), 117–124.
Haesbaert, R. (2007). Concepções de territorio para entender a desterritorialização. En: M. Santos and B. K. Becker (Org.). *Território, territórios: ensayos sobre o ordenamento territorial*, pp. 43–71. Third ed. Lamparina.
Haesbaert, R. (2009). Dilema de conceitos: espaço-território e contenção territorial. En: M. Saquet and E. Sposito (Orgs.). *Territórios e territorialidades: teorias, processos e conflitos*, pp. 95–120. Expresão Popular.
Haesbaert, R. (2013). Del mito de la desterritorialización a la multiterritorialidad. *Cultura y representaciones sociales* [Preprint].

Haesbaert, R. (2018). De categoria de análise a categoria da prática: a multiplicidade do territorio numa perspectiva latino-americana. En: F. Fridman, L.A. Gennari and S. Lencioni (Eds.). *Políticas públicas e territorios: onze estudos latino-americanos*, pp. 267–288. CLACSO. https://doi.org/10.2307/j.ctvnp0jdb.14
Haesbaert, R. (2019). Regional-global. Dilemas de la región y de la regionalización en la geografía contemporánea. *Locale.* doi: 10.14409/rl.v4i4.9804
Haesbaert, R. (2020). Território(s) numa perspectiva latino-americana. *Journal of Latin American Geography*, 19(1), 141–151. Available at: https://doi.org/10.1353/lag.2020.0007
Halvorsen, S. (2019). Decolonising territory: Dialogues with Latin American knowledges and grassroots strategies. *Progress in Human Geography*, 43(5), 790–814. Available at: https://doi.org/10.1177/0309132518777623
Harvey, D. (2004). *El nuevo imperialismo* (Vol. 26). Ediciones Akal.
Hernández Fonseca, J.C., and Fl Ivette Elizondo-Porras. (2006). Estudio sobre la adopción de variedades mejoradas de frijol en las principales zonas productoras de frijol de la región Brunca de Costa Rica, *Agronomía Mesoamericana*, 17(3), 357–367.
Herner, M.T. (2009). Territorio, desterritorialización y reterritorialización: un abordaje teórico desde la perspectiva de Deleuze y Guattari. *Huellas*, 13, 158–171.
Hidalgo, F., and Márquez-Fernández, Á. (2012). *Contrahegemonia y Buen Vivir.* Venezuela: Universidad Central del Ecuador y Universidad del Zulia.
Hope, D., and Limberg, J. (2020). *The economic consequences of major tax cuts for the rich.* International Inequalities Institute Working Papers (55). UK: London School of Economics and Political Science. http://eprints.lse.ac.uk/id/eprint/107919
Irarrázaval, F. (2018). Territorialidades: La 'Era del Gas Natural' En Peru y Bolivia, *Revista de geografía latinoamericana*, 17(3), 153–182.
Jessop, B. (2013). Hollowing out the 'nation-state' and multi-level governance. In: *A Handbook of Comparative Social Policy*, Second Edition (pp. 11–26). Edward Elgar Publishing.
Kingstone, P. (2018). *The Political Economy of Latin America: Reflections on Neoliberalism and Development after the Commodity Boom*. Second ed. Routledge. https://doi.org/10.4324/9781315682877
Larson, A.M. et al. (2016). The challenge of "Territory": Weaving the social fabric of indigenous communities in Nicaragua's Northern Caribbean Autonomous Region. *Bulletin of Latin American Research*, 35(3), 322–337.
Lefebvre, H. (1991). *The production of space.* Blackwell.
Liverman, D., and Vilas, S. (2006). Neoliberalism and the Environment, *Latin America Annual Review of Environment and Resources*, 31(1), 327–363. https://doi.org/10.1146/annurev.energy.29.102403.140729
López Sandoval, M., Robertsdotter, A., and Paredes, M. (2017). Space, Power, and Locality: The Contemporary Use of Territorio in Latin American Geography, *Journal of Latin American Geography*, 16(1), 43–67.
MacKinnon, D. and Cumbers, A. (2018). *An introduction to economic geography: Globalisation, uneven development and place.* Routledge.
Maldonado Valera, C., Tromben Rojas, V., Cea, C., and Suárez Sarrazin, J. (2021). *Panorama de la cohesión social en América Latina y el Caribe.* Comisión Económica para América Latina y el Caribe (CEPAL).
Maldonado-Torres, N. (2008). La descolonización y el giro des-colonial, *Tabula Rasa*, 9, 61–72.
Mançano, B. (2009). Sobre a tipologia de territórios. *Territórios e territorialidades: teorias, processos e conflitos*, 197–215.
Manzanal, M. (2007). Territory, Power and Institutions. A critical perspective. In: M. Manzanal, M. Archers, and B. Nussbaumer, (comp.). *Territories in Construction, Actors, plots and governments, between cooperation and conflict*, pp. 15–50. CICCUS.

Mardones Barrera, R. (2016). Discurso del territorio enunciado por las ciencias sociales en las publicaciones científicas de revistas latinoamericanas, *Prismasocial-Revista de Ciencias*, 16, 556–596.

Martin, R. and Sunley, P. (1998). Slow convergence? The new endogenous growth theory and regional development. *Economic Geography*, 74(3), 201–227.

Martínez Valle, L. (2012). Apuntes para pensar el territorio desde una dimensión social, *Ciências Sociais Unisinos*, 48(1), 12–18.

Mazurek, H. (2006). *Espacio y territorio. Instrumentos metodológicos de investigación social.* U-PIEB.

Medeiros, R. (2008). Territorio, espacio de identidade. En: M. Saquet and E. Sposito, (Eds.), *Territórios e territorialidades: Teorias, processos e conflitos*, pp. 217–228. UNESP.

Ministerio de Economía, Industria y Comercio. (2011). *Comercialización de Agroquímicos en Costa Rica.* Dirección de Estudios Económicos. http://www.infoagro.go.cr/Documents/Estudio%20de%20mercado%20de%20agroquimicos_meic_final.pdf

Morales, D., Sariego-Kluge, L., and Teixeira, T. (2024). Territories as Practice for economic transformations. Insights from Latin American geography, *Geoforum*, 154. doi.org/10.1016/j.geoforum.2024.104062

Murphy, J.T. (2008) Economic geographies of the global south: Missed opportunities and promising intersections with development studies. *Geography Compass*, 2(3), 851–873. Available at: https://doi.org/10.1111/j.1749-8198.2008.00119.x

Ōmae, K.I. and Ohmae, K. (1995). *The end of the nation state: The rise of regional economies.* Simon and Schuster.

Painter, J. (2010) 'Rethinking territory', *Antipode*, 42(5), 1090–1118.

Pollard, J. et al. (2009). Economic geography under postcolonial scrutiny. *Transactions of the Institute of British Geographers*, 34(2), 137–142. Available at: https://doi.org/10.1111/j.1475-5661.2009.00336.x

Pomareda, F. (2022, 18 de mayo). PNUD: Costa Rica usa 8 veces más plaguicidas que los demás países OCDE de América. *Semanario Universidad*, 2417.

Quimbayo Ruiz, G.A. (2020). Territory, sustainability, and beyond: Latin American urbanization through a political ecology. *Environment and Planning E: Nature and Space*, 3(3), 786–809. Available at: https://doi.org/10.1177/2514848619887933

Radcliffe, S.A. (2005). Development and geography: Towards a postcolonial development geography? *Progress in Human Geography*, 29(3), 291–298.

Raffestin, C. [1980]1993. *Por uma Geografia do poder.* Ática.

Rasmussen, M.B., and Lund, C. (2018). Reconfigurando los espacios fronterizos: la territorialización del control de los recursos. *Desarrollo mundial*, 101, 388–399.

Rodríguez-Pose, A. (2018). The revenge of the places that don't matter (and what to do about it). *Cambridge Journal of Regions, Economy and Society*, 11(1), 189–209. Available at: https://doi.org/10.1093/cjres/rsx024

Rosenman, E., Loomis, J. and Kay, K. (2020). Diversity, representation, and the limits of engaged pluralism in (economic) geography. *Progress in Human Geography*, 44(3), 510–533. Available at: https://doi.org/10.1177/0309132519833453

Rua, J. (2008). Desenvolvimento e Sustentabilidades: uma perspectiva geográfica. En: M.P. de Oliveira, M.C.N. Coelho, and A. de M. Corrêa, (orgs.), *O Brasil, A América Latina eo Mundo: espacialidades contemporâneas (1)*, pp. 387–400. Lamparina, Anpege, Faperj.

Santos, M. (1996). *A Natureza do Espaço.* São Paulo: Hucitec/Edusp.

Saquet, M. (2005). A relação espaço-tempo e a apreensão do movimento em estudos territoriais. En: *Encontro de Geógrafos da América Latina*, 10. Anais.

Saquet, M. and Sposito, E.S. (eds). (2009). *Territórios e territorialidades: teorias, processos e conflitos.* São Paulo: Expressão Popular.

Scott, A.J. and Storper, M. (2007). Regions, Globalization, Development. *Regional Studies*, 41(1), 191–205.

Sheppard, E., Barnes, T.J. and Peck, J., (2012). The long decade: Economic geography, unbound. In *The Wiley-Blackwell companion to economic geography*, 1–24.

Storper, M. (1997). *The regional world: Territorial development in a global economy*. New York and London: Guilford Press.

Svampa, M. (2015). Commodities Consensus: Neoextractivism and Enclosure of the Commons in Latin America. *South Atlantic Quarterly*, 114(1), 65–82. Available at: https://doi.org/10.1215/00382876-2831290

Swyngedouw, E.A. (1992). Territorial organization and the space/technology nexus. *Transactions of the institute of British Geographers*, 417–433.

Vázquez-Barquero, A. and Rodríguez-Cohard, J.C. (2019). Local development in a global world: Challenges and opportunities. *Regional Science Policy & Practice*, 11(6), 885–897. Available at: https://doi.org/10.1111/rsp3.12164

4 Territories and grassroot (de)velopment

Contributions to a popular, decolonial, and counterhegemonic research agenda

Marcos Aurelio Saquet and Pamela Cichoski

Introduction

In this chapter, we contribute to the debate on (de)velopment/involvement and territory by identifying problems in the literature used to explain our Latin American region. Our perspective shall be read as directed to the academic and research practice, from and for our universities. We highlight the limitations of the arguments put forth by David Harvey, Amartya Sen, and Boaventura de Sousa Santos. These arguments are insufficient to explain the dynamics of class struggle or to identify mechanisms for political and cultural emancipation in the context of colonial processes in Latin America and other regions of the Global South.

This insufficiency can be addressed by acknowledging that both science and popular knowledge are fundamental for studying, understanding, explaining, interpreting, and changing a specific historical reality from within, conditioning consciousness and praxis as historical determinations (Quijano, 1981; Saquet, 2017b, 2018, 2020, 2022). Based on the above, we ask: How can we understand the territory and relate it to the processes of territorial (de)velopment through cooperative, participatory action research (PAR) with the people in Latin America?

Based on 25 years of experience researching and working with grassroot territorial (de)velopment and using PAR methodology in the state of Paraná, Brazil, we argue that is possible to understand, represent, explain, and value our cultures and ecosystems scientifically and politically. Our approach allows co-constructing a process of territorial transformation from a participatory, dialogic, popular, reflexive, and sustainable perspective. Therefore, we propose the praxis of "place consciousness" to understand territories as spaces for self-organisation, political formation, mobilisation, struggle, confrontation, and action. Actions, policies, programmes and projects can be decolonial, aligning with our commitment to the causes and needs of the people.

DOI: 10.4324/9781032650241-5

We begin with the premise that geography is a social and inherently political science. Hence, its theories, methods, techniques, and concepts are not neutral; instead, they carry scientific-philosophical and political meaning based on the choices of each researcher or research group. Geography should increasingly become a decolonial, popular, and territorial science, producing knowledge that benefits society, especially for the popular classes involved in counterhegemonic and grassroots territorial processes.

The five basic concepts that have been fundamental to geography over the decades—space, region, place, landscape, and territory— have been continually redefined across different countries, changing the discipline's evolving approaches and concepts. In line with the objectives of each research and action project undertaken by our Territorial Studies Group at the State University of Western Paraná, Brazil, since 2002, we have selected key concepts to guide PAR. While acknowledging all five, we primarily focus on landscape and territory, paying attention to how these have been redefined over time by virtue of the themes, objectives, and issues of each research project and territorial action.

Territory has been a fundamental concept in our work, understood through trans-temporal, trans-scalar, and pluri-dimensional perspectives (Saquet 2015, 2019a [2007], 2019b, 2020, 2021). Through insights derived from each PAR project since 2002, we have expanded and refined our understanding of territory and (de)velopment, concluding that they emerge from the relationships between society, nature, time, and space, which influence the reproduction of our social, natural, and spiritual lives. Territory is invariably composed of various networks of circulation and communication—nodes, networks, and meshes; natural elements (soils, waters, vegetation, climates, etc.); diverse identities (economic, political, cultural, and environmental); and different power relations (economic, political, cultural, and environmental) that affect and are influenced by different appropriations of space, domination, hegemonies, and cosmologies, which are characterised by resistance, confrontations, struggles, and counterhegemonies. Territory exists "within" the (dis)continuous spatiotemporal process of territorialisation, deterritorialisation, and reterritorialisation, which are relational, reticular, processual, historical, (im)material, and multi-dimensional (Raffestin, 1977, 1993 [1980], 1984; Saquet, 2017a, 2018, 2019a, 2015, 2020, 2021).

Territory, development, and heritage are closely interconnected. Development is a "territorial problem" that encompasses cultural, political, and economic processes, as well as historical and relational formations (Bagnasco, 1978). The territory becomes a space of self-organisation and political formation, mobilisation, struggle, and confrontation where public policies, programmes, and projects that can be grassroots, popular and decolonial are actionable. This is our theoretical and political stance, which we carry out in our daily praxis. However, there are other approaches to studying grassroots territorial (de)velopment:

i) Territory as a conceptual tool to study the heterogeneous realities in a space-time, analysing the forms, mechanisms, objectives and rhythms of cooperation (subjects, scales, policies, rationalities, philosophies, actions, etc.), appropriations, and conflicts. This approach produces critical knowledge about the territory without directing it to public and private actors.
ii) A focus on cooperation, producing knowledge about territorial contexts at different scales, directed towards local and/or regional (de)velopment/involvement. This approach can create knowledge useful for fostering cooperation among different subjects.

The approach we employ involves cooperation during the process of research and action in the territory. This approach is carried out in collaboration with various subjects (urban and/or rural, public and/or private), where knowledge is produced in a horizontal, participatory, and dialogical manner (Freire, 2011 [1996]; Saquet, 2014, 2022). Here, the concept of praxis is essential, with territoriality serving as both an analytical category and means of cooperation with subjects from the territories. This collaboration directly contributes to their political and cultural emancipation, as well as to environmental preservation.

In this context, we work from within the academy to contribute to the construction of a more just and ecological society. We do so through a decolonial and counterhegemonic conception of grassroot territorial (de)velopment, using PAR to co-generate solutions for communal life (Cichoski, 2021; Cichoski and Alves, 2019; Saquet, 2017b, 2018, 2019a, 2019b, 2020). To demonstrate the possibility of researching and collaborating directly with and for the people involved in each project, the following section critically examines the limits of Eurocentrism and universalism, highlighting the need for a paradigmatic shift (in theory and practice) fundamental for working for and with Latin American peoples. In the second section we emphasise the importance of "place consciousness" and its activation across different scales of cooperation, vital for self-organisation and popular action for the participatory and dialogic construction of knowledge and territorial (de)velopment at the grassroots. In the third section, we share lessons from the Territorial Studies Group's praxis in PAR to help alleviate or eliminate oppressive and subordinate dynamics and contribute to reordering power relations. This aims to foster territorialities and temporalities that enable a more just and ecological society, both now and in the future. Finally, we conclude the chapter with some closing remarks.

Between geography, economics, and sociology: Limits of Eurocentrism and universalism

Before presenting our research and cooperative/action praxis, it is essential to critically examine and challenge conceptions that are predominantly abstract, universalist, Eurocentric, economistic, and urban-centric. This critique is crucial for understanding our subversive, decolonial and counterhegemonic perspective on territory and de(velopment).

We start this critical examination with Harvey's perspective on development. Harvey's analysis of the compression of space and time illustrates the connection between development and modernity Harvey (1993 [1989]). According to his argument, capital annihilates space through the fluidity and immediacy inherent in accelerated capital accumulation. This process creates fragmentation and inequality within extensive and densely connected global networks. Capital accumulation is reproduced and sustained through a powerful and unified movement of global capital, influenced by large transnational companies and state-linked financial, industrial, and commercial entities. Consequently, resistances are challenged by the rapid, powerful, global, and unified expansion of capital, as well as by the influence of transnational corporations and the states that are connected to these financial, industrial, and commercial companies. In essence, global economic forces dominate, making political mobilisation of popular classes—which are almost absent in Harvey's analysis—extremely difficult.

This analysis, however, overlooks the diversity and complexity of daily life in both urban and rural areas, which seem absent from his view of the postmodern condition. Indeed, we argue that Harvey's argument remains confined to the urban, disregarding the diversity of people, groups, social classes, and temporalities, while neglecting rural areas. This urban-centric and universalist perspective is devoid of other subjects, community knowledge, territories, empiricism, and the possibility of dialogue. It fails to provide means for achieving political autonomy, social rights, and better life conditions for all. Who progressed, annihilated, and conquered space? Where and how do these subjects live? There are many questions without answers in universalist approaches such as Harvey's, which prioritise economic-cultural globalisation obscuring, or annihilating, the forces of the subjects, popular classes, native peoples, places and territory, as also does Amartya Sen.

In this path of universalist and Eurocentric reflexion, Sen (2000 [1999]), despite his valuable contribution in framing development as freedom, presents a perspective that remains primarily focused on a political-economic conception. As a result, his framework lacks the depth and complexity (multidimensionality) required to fully grasp the social and environmental problems of daily life in Latin America and other continents. We align with Acosta (2016 [2012]), who argues that Amartya Sen does not question capitalism and the concurrent production of value as capital.

In our view, Sen's framework (2000 [1999]) reinforces the centrality of the "modern world" through a universalist, rationalist, and Eurocentric narrative. It seems inhumane that people must endure extremely precarious conditions and low wages merely to free themselves from the labour–capital relationship. Is it possible to create a less destructive globalisation? If so, how? Who is constructing or will construct the version of globalisation narrated by Amartya Sen? Is capitalist wage labour the only viable way of life in today's world?

Once again, we find unanswered questions that emerge when we engage with local communities in our research through a territorial (im)material popular praxis, carried out both inside and outside the university. This critique also occurs in the theoretical discussions of important postmodern researchers, such as Sousa Santos (2006), through his "Sociology of Absences" and "Sociology of Emergences". For Souza Santos, within the framework of the "Ecology of Knowledge", it is possible to recognise, make visible, and validate the diversity of knowledges and practices that exist in the world. These knowledges need to be self-recognised and interconnected/articulated independently of each other and of "translation" (political, emotional, and intellectual) (Souza Santos, 2006).

"Translation" is central to his theoretical argument and refers to the interpretation of diverse and multiple forms of knowledge, meaning rendering them intelligible to create potential agreements and articulations between different social movements, identifying similarities and differences that can be utilised for resistance and struggle. In the concept of "translation", the focus lies on subjects, practices, and knowledges, defining those practices with the greatest potential for counterhegemonic struggle.

Theoretically, the cognitive and political processes upheld by Sousa Santos (2006) are interlinked through a structured pedagogical sequence. However, we still observe a clear reproduction of Eurocentric, globalising, and universalist principles, as illustrated below:

a) The perpetuation of the dichotomy between "scientific knowledge" and "non-scientific knowledge", "modern knowledge" and "indigenous knowledge", in favour of a supposed "superiority of modern science": a profound issue at the theoretical, methodological, and political levels, as in practice it contributes to the marginalisation of subjects, groups, classes, and peoples;
b) The defence of "translating" distinct philosophies to reinforce his argumentation, such as Indian and African (which differ from one another and from "modernist" and "postmodernist" frameworks) risks inducing interpretations that may diverge significantly when carried out by Afro-descendant and/or Amerindian subjects;
c) The essentially subjective and personal meaning of his proposal for "translation", which, based on this typically intellectual endeavour, can

easily interfere with the course of decisions that are to be made, thereby producing other hegemonic forms of knowledge. It is also evident that "translation" favours those subjects who are most rhetorically skilful;

d) The neglect or lack of attention regarding the possibility of co-producing knowledge at a participatory, horizontal, symmetrical and dialogic level, in which the "crossing", "convergence", and "aggregation" of knowledges is advocated by certain subjects. This procedure, no matter how careful and responsible it may be, is inadequate for a popular, participatory, decolonial, and counterhegemonic pedagogy;

e) The insistence on the possibility of constructing a "counterhegemonic globalisation" that is almost entirely devoid of theoretical, methodological and empirical substance—that is, empty in relation to its necessary revolutionary praxis.

Unanswered questions persist here too: How can Souza Santos's (2006) approach effectively generate a viable alternative for people to live better? How can his "Sociology of Emergencies", "translation", and "ecology of knowledge" directly contribute to solving the everyday problems of people and communities?

The contributions made by David Harvey, Amartya Sen, and Boaventura de Sousa Santos certainly offer important theoretical and political insights. However, they remain insufficient to explain the class struggle and guide the political-cultural emancipation needed in Latin America and other continents. These authors' concepts do not sufficiently challenge the reproduction of social domination and dependencies of the local on the global, of the subaltern on the centre (Europe and North America), of the rural on the urban. These approaches are not truly connected with liberation and emancipation, nor with achieving the decision-making autonomy of the most impoverished and historically and geographically oppressed subjects.

The three selected authors remain immersed in their inward intellectual efforts, which are connected to the agents of transnational and globalising capital. Their contributions lack the necessary paradigmatic shift, both theoretical and practical, to effectively be adopted in our work with and for Latin American peoples. The conceptualisations of David Harvey, Amartya Sen, and Boaventura de Sousa Santos ultimately contribute to perpetuating the fetish of commodities, equality, visibility, freedom, and globalisation. They tend to replace human agency (broadly defined across various identities) with concepts like translations, commercial transactions, large networks, and development indices, among others.

In our view, scientific concepts, and the practices of territorial (de)velopment must be constructed in a way that involves popular participation. With such considerations and by being sensible to the vulnerability of communities, our research and collaboration move to a different direction. It involves immersing ourselves and committing to the subjects being studied, deeply rooted in cooperation and co-producing knowledge, based on specific places, individuals, and territories, while not neglecting the trans-scalar aspects of daily lives.

Class and place consciousness in the territory: Vital mediation for decolonisation and popular counterhegemony

Our experience in territorial research and action clearly reveals that we need to contribute systematically and directly to enhancing, practising, and expanding the level of "place consciousness", activating territorialities at different scales of cooperation, from urban neighbourhoods to rural communities, as we have already empirically and reflexively demonstrated in Saquet (2017a, 2017b, 2018, 2020, 2022). Our research and actions reveal that political mobilisation based on class consciousness alone is insufficient to solve the problems of the Brazilian people and of Latin Americans in general.

Given that territory and (de)velopment/involvement are intertwined and multidimensional—encompassing political, legal, social, environmental, and cultural dimensions, with tensions and disputes, struggles and appropriations, with varied worldviews and identities (Bustos Velazco, 2015), "place consciousness" has proven to be fundamental in the self-organisation (including ours, as researchers) and popular action in favour of participatory and dialogical constructions of knowledge and life projects. This consciousness allows for the expansion of social movements of resistance, demand, and struggle by working together in scientific research and popular cooperation, grounded in the singularities of each place.

"Place consciousness" is vital for identification and social participation, for the reproduction of place as a territory of coexistence with community relations, which can mean a possible antidote to economic globalisation (Becattini and Magnaghi, 2015; Saquet, 2017a, 2017b, 2020). Through "place consciousness", we remain immersed and committed to urban and/or rural neighbours, to the residents of the neighbourhoods where we study, work and live, as well as to our fellow students or work colleagues. This means living and acting within each territory of daily life, teaching and learning, researching and acting, and cooperating to solve people's problems in their territories.

Therefore, theory and practice are not separated. Science and popular knowledge are essential to study, understand, explain, interpret, and change a historical and geographical reality from within, conditioning consciousness and praxis as historical determinations (Quijano, 1981). In our praxis, research and cooperation/action at the root of territorial (de)velopment is built with different subjects, their knowledge, techniques and technologies adapted to each territory, time and place, and this process requires a continuous movement of political and cultural (in)formation, of co-production of common territorial solutions. Science and popular knowledge are mutually recognised and integrated to enhance our decolonial and counterhegemonic praxis in the processes of grassroots territorial (de)velopment.

We have learned this understanding at a theoretical level from researchers and activists from different countries and areas of knowledge, starting with the recognition of the sense of belonging to a "social class and a place" (Becattini, 2000 [1989], 2009; Magnaghi, 2000, 2006, 2011, 2013; Quaini, 2010) in a movement against the expanded reproduction of capital and environmental degradation, and in favour of ecological management in agriculture, the valorisation of popular knowledge, of historically constructed cultures, of crafts, of small businesses, in short, of life.

In this way, we contribute concretely to the decolonisation of our minds and everyday practices. Decolonisation occurs in a contradictory movement of subversion and counterhegemony. It is understood as a process aimed at creating a "new man" through the struggle for liberation (Fanon, 2005 [1961]). People in (im)material conditions of freedom to sow and eat, to transform and appropriate the results of their work, to sing and dance, to walk and teach, to learn and live, to feel safe and be healthy, to think and produce knowledge according to each territory and its people.

Thus, (I) the decolonial response will be ethical, social, political, and epistemic, based on an "other way of thinking" and a praxis that is also "other" (Walsh, 2014 [2008]). Decoloniality corresponds to a fight against coloniality and its "material, epistemic and symbolic effects", such as the naturalisation of extermination, domination, subordination, expropriation of lands, death, torture, rape, colonisation of thought, etc. (Maldonado-Torres, 2018). Therefore, decolonisation and decoloniality correspond to a process of contestation in favour of a radical break with hegemony and coloniality in people's mentality, so that it is, in fact, a "decolonial consciousness" (Maldonado-Torres, 2008). There are many discourses, not usually accompanied, however, by a practice consistent with the theoretical arguments.

In this way (II), we also contribute to the co-construction of a "counterhegemonic paradigm", contrary to Eurocentric and colonial capitalism (Hidalgo and Fernández, 2012), by combining knowledge and expertise, practices and theories in a process of socialisation and territorial transformation, which is autonomous, supportive, participatory, horizontal, reflexive, and popular to try to break with global economic, political, cultural and environmental degradation dependencies.

It is not about "hierarchising", "aggregating", and "translating" knowledge, nor about building economic and sectoral, urban, and globalising public policies, nor about any neoliberal, "modernist", or "postmodernist" project. It is not, therefore, a question of importing theories, concepts, models, narratives, etc., since this way of working directly contributes to reproducing our dependence on a "field of power" that is also intellectual and cultural, on the fetish of the commodity and, on a more general level, on "modern" and "postmodern" life, which ends up generating other invisibilities, dichotomies, and submissions, without the necessary rupture that could benefit Latin American peoples (Acosta, 2008). We increasingly need, without neglecting transnational dialogue, to co-produce our theories, arguments, research and action techniques, as well as public policies, produced for and with our people. Our problems, our solutions.

Our learnings about participatory action research in grassroots local territorial (de)velopment

Our praxis of research and cooperation, based on place awareness, has generated many useful lessons for the construction of public policies, programmes, and projects for grassroots territorial (de)velopment, built in a participatory and dialogical way and based on the singularities of each territory. Thus, it is necessary and possible to investigate, with our social and territorial immersion, in singular ecosystems, with people, cultures, knowledge, cosmologies, techniques, memories, needs, rhythms, etc., in accordance with the objectives of each project, integrating science and popular knowledge, and in a decolonial and counterhegemonic perspective. We do not "translate" or "cross" knowledge and practices: we strive, in each project, to co-produce knowledge, in a praxis that is as horizontal and dialogical as possible, as can be seen in detail in Saquet and Duarte (1996) and in Saquet (2018, 2019a, 2019b, 2020, 2022).

Thus, considering fundamental references such as Paulo Freire and Orlando Fals Borda, as well as the lessons learned from everyday experiences—we learn a lot by doing—we (im)materialise the PAR carried out through different techniques and research phases, successive and coexisting, which are summarised below:

1. Meetings and debates with different subjects interested in jointly building processes of social transformation: willingness is a fundamental premise. Subjects from the countryside and/or the city, such as peasants, workers, landless, unemployed, teachers, researchers, students, trade unionists, in short, different subjects meet to discuss and co-construct each participatory action research project, valuing the subject–subject relationship, in all phases and activities carried out by the researchers and the "researched" (the popular subjects of each project).
2. Formation of interdisciplinary (multidimensional) and interinstitutional teams, made up of NGOs, rural and urban workers' unions, workers' and residents' associations (urban and rural), schools (at different levels of training), churches, youth groups, mothers' clubs, and other state agencies.

3 Socialisations and debates on concepts, procedures, and research and action techniques, through colloquia, meetings, workshops, and seminars, also defining the forms of communication that would be used in each urban and /or rural development project.
4 Definition of coordination for each project and setting of planning actions, implementation of actions and evaluation, in the most horizontal, transparent, interdisciplinary, and interinstitutional way possible. Normally we work with general territorial and thematic coordination teams. The general ones coordinate the smaller teams and the entire action-research process; the territorial ones act more decisively in urban streets and/or rural towns; the thematic ones act on specific issues such as rural education, basic sanitation, public lighting, popular housing, etc.
5 Drafting of each urban and/or rural project: in some cases within the academic field (especially when there are calls from governments with short deadlines); in others, "within" a peasant and/or workers' social movement of resistance and struggle, socialising and debating the objectives, procedures, stages, and actions with the different themes of each project.
6 Debate and definition of research techniques and instruments with the participation of the population in interest. Our experience and learning reveal that the greater the participation of the people who will be the subjects of each project, the greater the commitments assumed and fulfilled. Our immersion and popular social participation are essential in each place, cooperating either to understand reality, to represent it, or to transform it according to the needs of the subjects of each project. The peasant or worker identity is a condition for social participation, but the same identity with a sense of class, which can be created due to existing struggles, is strengthened.
7 Collection and analysis of primary data (questionnaires, interviews, social mapping, photographic records, etc.), with the direct participation of the coordinating team, inter-institutional collaborators and at least some residents of the research action territory, co-producing the local diagnosis for presentation to the residents, discussion, and evaluation. Socialisation and debate correspond to the so-called "data feedback", which serves as a basis for discussion and for the participatory construction of the action/cooperation plan for each project. Workshops are always important in qualitative research and in participatory action: we inform, we learn, we theorise, and we practice, in short, it is a moment of a process of decolonial praxis.

8 Thus, thematic workshops, theoretical-practical field days and social cartography are highlighted as (in)formative activities and can be part of participatory research and/or participatory actions (Figure 4.1) in the university-territory unit.
9 Planning, analysis, and evaluation meetings for each project carried out. They must be dispersed and articulated territorially, in the same movement of integration, mobilisation and work, also serving as a basis for debates and for (re)defining action plans.
10 Debate and deliberation assemblies, held to define the priorities of each action plan: what will be carried out, how, where, who, when, financial and logistical resources needed. These are essential moments of social participation, immersion, political commitment and autonomy by urban and rural communities. Assemblies are territorial nodes of political decision, awareness of place and praxis of popular struggle as we carry out our participatory action research projects. In this way we are always stronger, with collective decisions used to achieve what the subjects of each project need.
11 Mobilisation and organisation of actions of vindication, resistance and struggle, collaborating directly in the solution of the problems identified in each territory and time, also trying to qualify the levels of class and place consciousness, individual and collective commitments, solidarity, learning, relationships of trust, etc.
12 Participatory, respectful, analytical and evaluative monitoring, practising the action–reflection–action relationship, redoing and adjusting what is necessary to achieve the objectives and goals of each project, considering the principles of participation, autonomy in decision-making, solidarity, cooperation, interdisciplinarity, inter-institutionality, sustainability, and counterhegemony.
13 Production of popular and territorial knowledge for solving the problems of subjects in their territories: some published in scientific journals; others, in illustrated information brochures for the local population. This can occur at three main levels: a) in teams, with the participation of different researchers and "researched" subjects; b) in teams, among researchers; c) among popular subjects (Saquet, 2019a, 2019b, 2020, 2021). The production of knowledge in our projects assumes the characteristics of each team. Of course, we always have scientific objectives by academically socialising our experiences, however, we are always attentive to the needs of the subjects of each project, adapting texts and publications to their most urgent needs. Normally, this construction involves students, political leaders, teachers and peasants, men and women; the research, analysis and writing work is carried out in popular territories and at the university (which is also a territory).

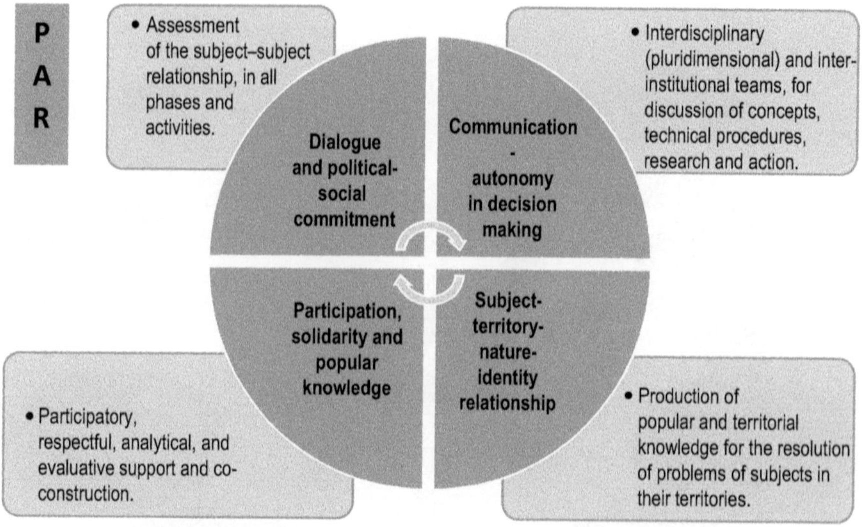

Figure 4.1 The construction of grassroot territorial (de)velopment with class and place consciousness.

Source: Cichoski e Saquet, 2021.

In this way, we are practising PAR inside and outside the university, in urban neighbourhoods and rural communities, in streets and farms, valuing different subjects, interdisciplinary teams, inter-institutionality, dialogues, action–reflection, and the socialisation of learning in the direction of a territorial and popular science. In this way, we also believe that we are contributing a little to the broader movement of decolonisation of our minds and practices. (Figure 4.1).

Eviently, during our projects of research and territorial action, we have encountered many difficulties. The slowness in gaining the trust of the subjects with whom we would like to work; the bureaucracy of state institutions (especially in financial banks); having to adapt specific techniques and technologies; to territorial singularities; lack of public funding for health, sanitation, public security, and research; and dealing with the phases of Brazilian the State of Paraná politics. These aspects, among others, are difficult obstacles to overcome. Often, however, they also end up motivating political-cultural encounter and unity in favour of the popular classes, strengthening self-organisation, class and place consciousness, as well as relations of reciprocity, thus producing energies of solidarity and cooperation based on the PAR methodology (Figure 4.2)

We argue that PAR has a central role as a popular methodology that is necessarily participatory, dialogical and territorial. It is impossible for us to share and cooperate without being in the territories of our most vulnerable people. We can cooperate from a distance (virtually), but the PAR is a process

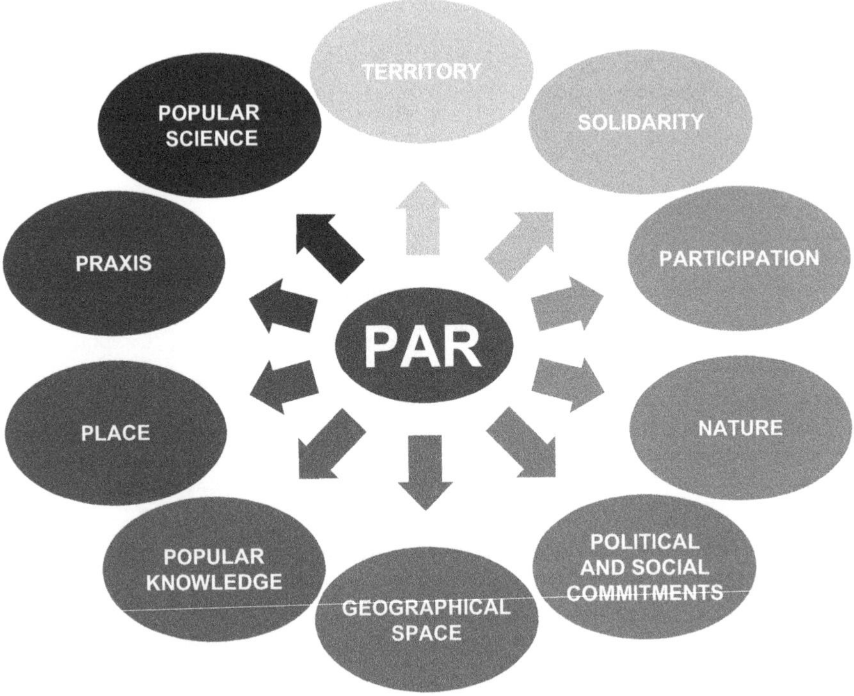

Figure 4.2 The centrality of PAR in decoloniality and territorial cooperation.

Source: Cichoski e Saquet, 2021.

of social and territorial immersion, of face-to-face co-production of knowledge and of popular solutions made personally. It is possible for personal, everyday life activities to coexist with other remote/virtual ones, and this must be defined by each PAR team. We are in the territories, with the people, practising solidarity in a territorial and popular geography as we have already shown.

For this reason, we believe that PAR is current, relevant, and appropriate, both scientifically and popularly. We are conditioned to look at and focus our research and actions with people, in ecosystems, considering life and daily rhythms, techniques and popular knowledge, cooperating in the territories. As Melin, Mansilla Quiñones and Royo (2016) argue, through the PAR, the community's own knowledge, feelings and thoughts are valued.

We agree with Bozanno and Canevari (2020) regarding respectful, dialogic interactions between different people and knowledges at the community and territorial levels; as they reinforce the need for a multidimensional (cultural, psychological, economic, political, and natural), trans-scalar, and normative territorial approach aimed at enhancing "territorial intelligence" (present in each territory) through a "dialogue of knowledge and practices".

It would seem very "intelligent" to identify, understand, represent, and explain the intelligences of subjects, their traditions, their techniques, routines, skills, desires, and needs, empowering them to live better, always achieving greater autonomy in decision-making, and social and environmental well-being.

This implies a very different conception of (de)velopment—which we call grassroot— with involvement that is necessarily communal (cooperation and solidarity), ecological, participatory, dialogical, popular, decolonial, and counter-hegemonic. In this way we can (im)materialise a popular territorial praxis, contributing with our research and other actions to lessen or eliminate oppressive, subordinate and dominant involvements; to rejoin a field of cooperation and solidarity, of sharing and synergy; co-constructing their own mobilisation, struggle, resistance, and their own knowledge based on the (territorial and humanitarian) heritage of each territory: praxis made with bodies and souls, sciences and emotions, technologies and cosmologies, from people, for and with them (Saquet, 2018, 2019a, 2019b, 2020, 2021).

Thus, there is a continuous effort to co-produce knowledge and other actions of resistance, struggle, and cooperation, to achieve what the local *campesinos* and neighbours of the urban periphery need, what our people need. Our geography is based on the local and the regional, on research and action. Although normally many researchers emphasise the global over the local, we emphasise the local without neglecting transnational and global relations and networks. This has proven to be fundamental for research and collaboration with popular subjects through a popular and territorial geography, of decision-making autonomy, self-organisation and proximity, achieved with cultural and territorial roots, with immersion, political commitment, and co-participation.

What we see in Brazilian (human) geography, for example, is the great predominance of national and international (or global) scales, to understand and explain local and/or regional processes. This, in our opinion, greatly impoverishes the apprehension and understanding of the object of study. Given that the analyses are general, globalising, universalising, etc., often homogenising spaces, places, territories, subjects, groups, classes and peoples, generating better knowledge for the "investigated" subjects becomes very difficult. Particularly so they can reorganise themselves politically, fight and live with increased wellbeing.

Despite the difficulties of working simultaneously in teaching, research and cooperation, our geography is also focused on the future, without disregarding the past and the present. This is also a fundamental lesson, so as to avoid falling into the old rhetoric of theoretical imitation of Eurocentric, universalist and urban-centric references; as well as not to reproduce historicist research that does not contribute to reordering power relations and producing territorialities and temporalities of a more just and ecological society, in the present and for the future.

Numerous colleagues research, mainly, past processes to try to understand and explain the present. We clearly know that past and present are not separate, but we must be sensitive to the emerging and very serious, causes of the poverty or misery in the daily lives of millions of people in Latin America (and billions if we consider other continents). Reviewing international literature and even global historical processes is of course important, however, we believe that this should be one of the means rather than being sole purpose, and thus neglecting or totally denying the existence of popular and ancestral knowledge, as well as the realities still deeply rooted in the territories.

In this way, in the geography of the territorial praxis that we carry out, of the future and of the place, of autonomy and proximity, the participatory community dimension is also fundamental as a spatial and temporal dimension of activation of territoriality for political mobilisation, for the co-production of knowledge, for the vindication, finally, of the horizontal construction of the root (un)development for and with the people. Democracy can effectively take place in the affirmation and strengthening of the community (Acosta, 2008).

The most recommended occasions to guide a projection of the future, such as strengthening the different linkages between identity, culture, synergy, organisational fabric, and territory, arise from the cultural and territorial dimensions of community life (Belliggiano and De Rubertis, 2012). The linkages precisely signify the different gradients of anchoring, proximity, trust, belonging, cooperation and solidarity, elements and processes that are central to the territorial characterisation of (un)development based on the singularities (social-natural-cosmological) of each territory.

This process drives us, during participatory action-research, to create other forms of democracy in communities for the care of the territory in a sustainable way in all its social and natural dimensions (Magnaghi, 2000, 2006, 2011; Lizárraga and Vacaflores, 2014), in an (im)materially popular and cooperative reflection-action. Being part of a community means immersion with commitment on our part, as researchers and collaborators, critics, and co-builders. This rootedness and proximity can occur in a neighbourhood or between different urban neighbourhoods, in a rural community, or even between the urban and the rural, always within a territorial scope.

Our historical praxis of participatory action-research also reveals that it is at the level of communities and territories that the possibilities of building a more just and ecological society (based on solidarity, neighbourhoods, and experiences) are debated and defined. This was also argued in a more general context, by Ceceña (2017), Maldonado-Torres (2018) and Dussel (1986) "Community life itself is an example of these exercises in democracy" (Acosta, 2016 [2012], p. 147). Therefore, in addition to qualitative and critical research, we consider vital to recreate reciprocity, cooperation, and solidarity, as presuppositions of life in the same territory—planet Earth.

Some final words

From our exposition in this text, starting from a brief problematisation of conceptions that we consider Eurocentric, universalist, urban-centric and globalising, as well as from the socialised synthesis of our action-research praxis, we hope that the reader will have clarity about the substantial differences that exist at the theoretical, methodological and political level, differences that result in another way of understanding science, the university, (im) material reality and acting in everyday life in a cooperative and supportive way with the most vulnerable populations.

The geography that we create and practice, as well as the philosophical guidelines that we use, are made in popular praxis, inside and outside the university, cohabiting and living as much as possible with the popular subjects who participate, despite the difficulties, in each phase of territorial research and action. The praxis needs to have the meaning of popular resistance, confrontation, political struggle, and the construction of autonomous management of territories through knowledge that influences the characterisation of the consciousness of place, based on what Fals Boda called reflection-action (1978, 1981). Thus, we can characterise, not our understanding, but a geography of and for cooperation aimed at the (un)development of the roots of the territory, carried out in everyday decolonial praxis, with our immersion and direct commitment to the popular classes (Saquet et al., 2012; Saquet, 2015, 2017a, 2017b, 2020, 2021).

Our praxis is anchored in regional culture, political self-organisation, and the singularities of each territory, its subjects, and ecosystems, which necessarily means proximity and reciprocity. Our territorial praxis is supportive, interactive, scientific, and popular, recognising that all subjects are beings who think and feel, breathe and eat, and possess valuable knowledge and experiences for the collaborative creation of solutions to everyday problems, which are often shared.

Bibliography

Acosta, Y. (2008). *Filosofía latinoamericana y democracia en clave de derechos humanos*. Montevideo: Editorial Nordan-Comunidad

Acosta, A. (2016 [2012]). *O bem vivir: an opportunity to imagine other worlds*. São Paulo: Autonomy Literária, Elefante.

Bagnasco, A. (1978). Problematiche dello sviluppo e artcolazione dell'analisi: un paradigma per l'analisi territoriale. In: A. Bagnasco, Messori, M. y Trigilia, C. (Org.). *Le problematiche dello sviluppo italiano*. Milão: Feltrinelli. pp. 205–251

Becattini, G. (2000 [1989]). *Dal 'setore' industriale al 'distretto' industriale. Alcune considerazioni sull'unità di indagine dell'economia*. Torino: Rosenberg & Sellier.

Becattini, G. (2009). *Ritorno al territorio*. Bologna: Il Mulino

Becattini, G. y Magnaghi, A. (2015). Coscienza di classe e coscienza di luogo. In: Becattini, G. (Org.). *La coscienza dei luoghi*. Roma: Donzelli. pp. 115–222

Belliggiano, A. y De Rubertis, S. (2012). Le filiere corte agroalimentari nei processi di sviluppo locale, *XXIV Convegno di Sinergie*. Lecce (Itália), 513–524

Bozanno, H., and Canevari, T. (2020). *Transform dialogues of knows into dialogues of dos. Science, community and public policies*. The Silver: EDULP/UNLP.
Bustos Velazco, E. (2015). Tendencias investigativas en territorio y su importancia en la formación de profesionales. *Revista LEBRET*, 7, 261–279
Ceceña, A. (2017). Poder, emancipación, guerra y sujetividad. In: León Hernández, E. (Org.). *Praxis espacial en América Latina*. Lo geopolítico puesto en cuestión. Ciudad de México: ITACA. pp. 21–60.
Cichoski, P. (2021). *Interdisciplinarity in research and participatory action*. Contributions by Orlando False Embroidery Rio de Janeiro, Consequence.
Cichoski, P., and Alves, A. (2019). A search for the work of Orlando Fals Borda: contributions to rethink rural development, *Revista Campo-Território*, 14 (34), 61–85.
Dussel, E. (1986). *Ética comunitária*. Petrópolis, RJ: Vozes
Fals Borda, O. (1978). By praxis: the problem of how to investigate reality to transform it. In: *Cartagena World Symposium*. Bogotá, Punta de Lanza. pp. 209–249
Fals Borda, O. (1981). Science and the people. In: F. Grossi, V. Gianotten, and T. Whit (Org.). *Participatory research and rural praxis*. Lima, Blue Fly. pp. 19–47.
Fals Borda, O. (2013a [2001]). Kaziyadu – registro del reciente despertar territorial en Colombia. In: *Orlando F. Borda – Socialismo raizal y el ordenamiento territorial*. Bogotá: Editorial Desde Abajo. pp. 137–218.
Fals Borda, O. (2013b [2007]). Hacia el socialismo raizal y otros escritos. In: *Orlando F. Borda – Socialismo raizal y el ordenamiento territorial*. Bogotá: Editorial Desde Abajo. pp. 35–136.
Fanon, F. (2005[1961]). *The condemned of the earth*. Fora Judge: Ed. UFJF.
Freire, P. (2011 [1996]). *Pedagogia da autonomia*. Saberes necessários à prática educativa. São Paulo, Paz e Terra
Harvey, D. (1993 [1989]). *In post-modern condition*. São Paulo: Loyola Publishing House.
Hidalgo, F. y Fernández, Á. (2012). *Contrahegemonia y buen vivir*. Venezuela: Universidad Central del Ecuador y Universidad del Zulia.
Lizárraga, P. y Vacaflores, C. (2014). Lo agrario en la reconstitución del sujeto indígena originario campesino. In: F. Hidalgo, F. Houtart y P. Lizárraga (Org.). *Agriculturas campesinas en Latinoamérica* – propuestas y desafíos. Quito: Editorial IAEN. pp. 277–296
Magnaghi, A. (2000). *The local project*. Turin: Bollati Boringhieri.
Magnaghi, A. (2006). From participation in the self-government of the local community: towards municipal federalism solidade, *Democracy and Law*, (3), 1–13.
Magnaghi, A. (2011). Educare al territorio: conoscere, rappresentare, curare, governare. In: Giorda, C. y Puttilli, M. (Org.). *Educare al territorio, educare il territorio - Geografia per la formazione*. Roma: Carocci. pp. 32–42
Magnaghi, A. (2013). Re-territorializing the world, *Territorial Sciences*, 1, 47–58.
Magnaghi, A. (2015). La lunga marcia del ritorno al territorio. In: Becattini, G. (Org.). *La coscienza dei luoghi*. Roma: Donzelli. pp. VII–XVI.
Maldonado-Torres, N. (2008). La decolonización y el giro des-colonial, *Tabula Rasa*, (9), 61–72.
Maldonado-Torres, N. (2018). Analítica da colonialidade e da decolonialidade: algumas dimensões básicas. In: J. Bernardino-Costa, N. Maldonado-Torres, R. Grosfoguel (Org.). *Decolonialidade e pensamento afrodiaspórico*. Belo Horizonte: Autêntica Editora. pp. 27–53.
Melin, M., Mansilla Quiñones, P., and Royo, M. (2016). *Mapu Chillkantukun Zugu: Descolonizando el Mapa del Wallmapu, Construyendo Cartografía Cultural en Territorio Mapuche*. PuLofMapuXawun Publishers.

Quaini, M. (2010). Dalla coscienza di classe alla "coscienza di luogo" ovvero "de la lutte des classes à la lutte des places". En: Fondazione Benetton. *Declinazioni del concetto di luogo e di paesaggio*, 1–13.

Quijano, A. (1981). *Reencuentro y debate: una introducción a Mariátegui*. Lima: Mosca Azul

Quijano, A. (2000). The ghost of desarrollo en América Latina, *Rev. Venezolana de Economía y Ciencias Sociales*, 6(2), 73–90.

Raffestin, C. (1977). Paysage et territorialitè, *Cahiers de géographie du Québec*, 21(53–54), 123–134.

Raffestin, C. (1984). Territorialization, deterritorialization, reterritorialization and information. In: A. Turco (Org.). *Region and regionalization*. Milan: Angeli. pp. 69–82.

Raffestin, C. (1993 [1980]). *Por uma geography do poder*. São Paulo: Ática.

Sánchez, A. (2004). Dilemas teóricos y metodológicos de la sociología rural en América Latina. *Revista ALASRU - Nueva Época*, 10, 359–380.

Saquet, F. (2018). A perspective of counter-hegemonic analysis and territorial transformation, *Geographica Helvetica*, 73, 347–355.

Saquet, M.; Duarte, V. (1996). Projeto Vida na Roça: da concepção ao plano de ação agropecuário. Francisco Beltrão: FACIBEL/ASSESOAR.

Saquet, M. (2014). Social participation in territories of identity and development in a dialogical and cooperative praxis. In: O. Silva, E. Santos, and A. Coelho Neto (Org.). *Identity, territory and resistance*. Rio de Janeiro: Consequence. pp. 11–36

Saquet, M. (2015). *For a geography of territorialities and temporalities: a multidimensional conception oriented towards cooperation and territorial development*. La Plata, Argentina: FAHCE/UNLP.

Saquet, M. (2017a). Territory, social class and place: fundamental premises of locally based, ecological and cultural territorial development, *Pereira - Colombia, Arquetipo*, 15, 39–69.

Saquet, M. (2017b). *Awareness of class and place, praxis and territorial development*. Rio de Janeiro: Editora Consequência.

Saquet, M. (2019a). *Approaches and conceptions of territory*. 2007 edition. Bogotá: Editorial Universidad Distrital Francisco José de Caldas.

Saquet, M. (2019b). Popular knowledge in territorial praxis: a possibility for working with people, *GEOTEMA Magazine – AGEI*, Supplement 2019, 5–16.

Saquet, M. (2019c). The territory: the territorial approach and its implications for development dynamics, *Report Gepec*, 23, 25–39.

Saquet, M. (2020). *Popular knowledge, territorial praxis and counter-hegemony*. Mexico City: ITACA Editorial.

Saquet, M. (2021). *Popular knowledge, territorial praxis and counter – hegemony*. Curitiba: Brazil Publishing.

Saquet, M. (2022). Por una praxis territorial popular: una perspectiva metodológica in(sub)versiva y decolonial. In: Rocha, A.; Saquet, M.; Grignoli, D. (Ed.). *Novos paradigmas e novos modelos de ação: do global ao local ou do local ao global?* Rio de Janeiro: Editora Letra Capital. pp. 14–42

Saquet, M., Dansero, E., and Candiotto, L. (Org.). (2012). *Geography of and for development cooperation territorial: Brazilian and Italian experiences*. SP: Other Expressions.

Sen, A. (2000 [1999]). *Desenvolvimento como liberdade*. São Paulo: Companhia das Letras

Sen, A. (2002). *Rationality and freedom*. Harvard University Press.

Sen, A. (2007). The capability approach. *Journal of Human Development*, 8.

Sousa Santos, B. (2006). *A grammar of time: for a new political culture*. São Paulo: Cortez.
Velazco, B., and Hernan, E. (2015). Research trends in territory and their importance in training professionals, *LEBRET Journal*, (7), 261–262.
Walsh, C. (2014[2008]). Interculturality and coloniality of power. A different thought and positioning from the colonial difference. In: W. Mignolo (Ed.). *Interculturality, decolonization of the State and knowledge*. Buenos Aires: Del Signo. pp. 17–51.

Part 2

Case studies

5 Dependency, food production, and territorialisation at the borders of capital in Argentina

Martín Nicolás Sotiru and Mariano Féliz

Introduction

Latin America is facing significant territorial transformations. These processes involve new forms of dependency that combine cycles of re-indebtedness on expanded and multi-scale extractivist economies. The new dependency produces deterritorialisation and reterritorialisation driven by financial capital, which attempts to advance in different territories while people resist and build alternatives. It is at the borders of these territories where confrontations between different logics of social reproduction occur.

We understand the territory as a material and symbolic framework of social relations, always intersected by power dynamics (Manzanal, 2007). This includes multiple inseparable dimensions: economic, social, political, environmental, cultural, and historical (Mançano Fernandes, 2011). Additionally, territory is a multi-scalar concept with processes that occur transversally at various scales (Ortiz, 1998). The multidimensionality and multiscalarity of territories allow us to account for the articulation between social, political, and economic changes in different locations within the global logic of capital. Under this lens, territorialisation is a process that (re)configures dependency in recent Argentina. Using the case of food production, we articulate dependency with the concepts of territory and border, showing how capital advances in a differentiated way (due to resistances) within countries, confronting different models of territorial development. To do this, we first address the relationship between the conditions of dependency and food production strategies in our territories. Then, we debate the meaning and relevance of territorialisation as processes of dispute and imposition of social power. Thirdly, we analyse the advance of agribusiness in Latin America and Argentina as a process of (re/de) territorialisation, pointing out agroecology as a resistance strategy, among other possible ones. Subsequently, we examine recent experiences in Argentina to provide elements about the appropriation/construction of the territory, as well as the implications for territorial development.

This is qualitative research aiming to account for the reconfiguration of dependency in Argentina based on the case of food production, highlighting some recent experiences that exemplify our approach. It is not the objective

DOI: 10.4324/9781032650241-7

of this work to indicate trends and/or results based on probabilistic sampling. The methodology includes a bibliographic review of the main concepts and an analysis of secondary sources, including specialised reports, series, and statistical information. For specific experiences, we add journalistic sources to capture the voices of these resistance processes and other relevant data.

Dependency and food

Capitalism articulates and constitutes different territories in an unequal chain of exploitation and valorisation. In the configuration of the dependency relationship, Latin America was positioned as a key area for the expanded reproduction of global capital (Marini, 2015). National states played a primary role in creating the material and subjective, economic, and legal conditions necessary for the new independent nations to become territories useful for the plundering of natural resources, contributing to the expanded valorisation of capital from the centre. Hence, dependency is created when territories that were centred on the reproduction of life, such as those of indigenous peoples, were (re)configured as dependent/peripheral territories to provide raw materials for central imperialist spaces (Marini, 2015).

Dependency has undergone a series of stages framed by crises and transitions in the cycles of global capitalist exploitation. These crises and transitions have included substantive transformations in the dynamics of global accumulation and social reproduction, and each transition has involved new developments in the organisation of food regimes (McMichael, 2006). A food regime refers to how food production is organised and articulated on a global scale. The food regime plays a key role in the organisation of capitalist social reproduction because producing quality food at adequate prices is essential for reproducing the labour force on a global scale, thus underpinning global capitalist exploitation (Patel and Moore, 2017).

The crises and transitions were accompanied by global conflicts and open disputes over the management of food production systems. During the era of the British Empire, dependent capitalism facilitated the consolidation of industrial capitalism in the core regions by reducing the costs of food production (Marini, 2015; McMichael, 2006, p. 275). The capitalist crisis of the 1930s altered dependency relations, leading to a transformation in food production and consumption towards a pattern of systemic integration. This period saw the emergence of an incipient agribusiness industry on a global scale and the consolidation of increasingly homogenised consumption patterns (McMichael, 2006, pp. 275–276). Concurrently, dependent territories experienced agricultural 'modernisation' and the onset of the Green Revolution, which accompanied fragmented and incomplete industrialisation processes in the periphery (Marini, 2015).

The neoliberal crisis of the 1970s intensified the transnationalisation of capital, leading to the establishment of global institutional frameworks such as the World Trade Organization, the World Bank, and the International Monetary Fund. The food regime evolved into a 'corporate' regime where transnational corporations dominate food production within a financialised global order (McMichael, 2006). Today, in the context of a civilisational crisis of capital, global agriculture (McMichael, 2006, pp. 285–286) intersects with a new geopolitical transition centred on China, which remains an area of contention.

Each crisis compels capital to expand its borders, seeking new territories to conquer. We conceptualise the border not only in a physical sense but also as social and political. Capital aims to push beyond these borders, reconfiguring territories and reshaping them socially, politically, and economically. In every crisis, capital must overcome the self-imposed barriers (Bell and Cleaver, 1982), temporally and spatially displacing its contradictions (Harvey, 2005) to recreate conditions for valorisation. These movements involve temporarily bypassing the limits of capital by forcefully penetrating new territories (Luxemburg, 2018).

Crises reveal not merely 'material' borders but fundamentally political ones. They highlight the impossibility of continuing the exploitation of labour and nature. Yet, this impossibility reflects a refusal to accept increasingly unsustainable conditions of exploitation (Caffentzis, 2013; Federici, 2018). In response to this barrier, which capital has imposed upon itself, the system attempts a leap into the void. In this leap, capital seeks to overcome its contradictions by initiating a broad reorganisation of exploitable territories. These territories are not only spatial but, fundamentally, subjective. Therefore, capital aims to (re)territorialise itself by developing new practices for the expanded reproduction of value. It strives to establish forms of life reproduction that are once again adequate for its valorisation. By adopting new production modalities, exploitation patterns, and strategies for extracting natural wealth and appropriating common goods, capital aims to create a leap forward. This leap seeks to temporarily evade the certainty of its own historical mortality.

From territory to (re/de)territorialisation

We define territory as a segment of geographical space that is appropriated (symbolically) and/or controlled (materially) by social actors who create and sustain it through the exercise of power. According to Entrena Durán (2010), territory is a socially differentiated space that functions as a 'scenario of action and social relations' (p. 703), where actions and relationships are shaped. These relationships are influenced by power, hence synthetising 'spatialized power relations' (Manzanal, 2007, p. 12). Consequently, power—a relational concept, or rather the exercise of power—is crucial for understanding and characterising territory. Castells (2009) suggests that power can be viewed as the capacity of an actor or group to impose their will and interests by influencing or controlling the decisions of others. This power can be exercised materially, for instance, by constructing barriers and controlling access, or symbolically, by establishing rules or norms (Blanco, 2010), which do not necessarily have to be formal, such as dictating the production methods or types of goods.

On the other hand, processes of territorialisation involve two simultaneous and inseparable dynamics: deterritorialisation and reterritorialisation. These processes can arise from territorial disputes, which occur when actors with differing, and often conflicting, territorial logics confront one another. As Entrena Durán (2010) explains, 'territorialization implies an appropriation of the natural-physical space by various social actors' (p. 704). Territorialisation reflects the projection of power relations among social actors within a space. These power relations can be interpreted as forms of solidarity, cooperation, and mutual support, or as mechanisms of appropriation, domination, and exploitation (Llanos-Hernández, 2010, p. 217).

Territorial disputes arise when the existence, persistence, and continuity of one territory depend on the displacement or disappearance of another. In this context, if one actor (or group) loses control or appropriation of their territory to another actor(s) who establishes their own territory, this results in the deterritorialisation of the former and the reterritorialisation of the latter (Haesbaert, 2011). Deterritorialisation can involve the direct expulsion of the 'original' actors or their subordination to a different logic, which may not require physical expulsion but involves the imposition of new rules, norms, or practices. This process necessitates the emergence of new actors who can enforce these changes. Deterritorialisation processes do not inherently have negative effects (Entrena Durán, 2010), just as reterritorialisation processes do not necessarily have positive effects. Entrena Durán (2010) observes that while deterritorialisation processes can lead to disintegration and conflict, reterritorialisation processes involve the restructuring of socio-economic functions and/or the symbolic-cultural redefinition of a territory.

The processes of deterritorialisation and reterritorialisation result in modifications to territorial borders. Borders are not always physical or clearly defined; what matters is the control and who wields it. This control can encompass access and usage of the territory, as well as the management of flows and connections between territories. Such processes can reconfigure dependency relationships. For instance, territories that were previously somewhat isolated from the global market can become directly integrated through the (re)territorialisation of a multinational agribusiness. The expansion of crops like soybeans 'reflects processes of breadth and manifestation on a global scale' (Manzanal, 2017, p. 8). Changes in territorial borders lead to a reorganisation of the territory, altering its position in the international division of labour and global exploitation chains. As global actors increase their presence in a territory, the ability of local actors to control the impacts of these actors' actions generally diminishes (Entrena Durán, 2010).

The (re)territorialisation of capital involves imposing its logic of valorisation on various territories. Conversely, the (re)territorialisation efforts of subaltern groups—such as the recovery of a closed factory by its former workers—represent the establishment of new solidarity relations and the deterritorialisation of previous ownership and traditional employer-employee dynamics. García Guerreiro and Wahren (2014) demonstrate that when social organisations and movements (re)territorialise, they often become 'more complex and innovative, creating alternative ways to approach and practice the economy, health, education, politics, culture, and more' (p. 307).

It is important to recognise that territorial disputes often reveal at least two opposing models of territorial development. The intersection of 'development' and 'territory' began gaining prominence in the 1980s and solidified in the 1990s with the concept of territorial development (Martínez Godoy and Clark, 2015). This concept has been particularly influential in public policies, offering a practical framework for analysing and influencing 'phenomena, processes, situations, and contexts occurring in specific spaces' (Schneider and Peyré Tartagua, 2006, p. 14). Schneider and Peyré Tartagua (2006) argue for a dialogue between the abstract notion of territory and more concrete approaches to rural development. They define rural development 'as a process resulting from coordinated actions aimed at fostering socio-economic and environmental changes in rural areas' (p. 18). They propose using the concept of territory to analyse social change processes and suggest focusing on two dimensions: 'the dynamics of social forms of work and production, and the processes of social organization and participation' (p. 20). The first dimension concerns the socio-economic processes of production and reproduction, while the second relates to the capacity of actors to transform the territory, whether through political organisation or other mechanisms of power.

Building on these ideas, we adopt a broad conception of development as a process aimed at transforming existing power relations (Manzanal, 2007, 2014). Madoery (2013) explains that the concept of development involves an epistemic dispute between different interpretations. One perspective emphasises economic priorities, maintaining capitalism, and viewing the market as the ideal environment for resolving social relations. This approach presents development as a technical issue within modernity. The other perspective prioritises politics by critiquing capitalist exploitation and modernity, rejecting linear progress, and recognising that societies are shaped by unequal power relations. This view advocates for constructing alternatives driven by anti-capitalist social groups.

According to this dual interpretation, territorial development encompasses two distinct meanings. On one hand, it involves integrating territories into global capital circuits, thereby (re)creating dependency. On the other hand, it involves building alternative projects centred on the reproduction of life and nature. The nature of territorial development will depend on the social actors driving these processes. Saquet (2021) concludes that 'development is territorial and encompasses transformations and issues that persist, including traditions, identities, relationships of belonging and trust, networks of cooperation and productive specialization, as well as competition and domination' (p. 26). Therefore, territorial development models are always contingent, subject to disputes, and open to modifications.

Agribusinesses and (re/de)territorialisation in Latin America

In recent decades, the expansion of agribusiness in Latin America has transformed peasant and indigenous territories into platforms for profit extraction and commodity export, fuelling global chains of exploitation and dependence. The most prominent example of this transformation is the extensive monoculture of crops such as soybeans, corn, palm oil, sunflower, sugar cane, and forestry. The impact on local producers varies: some small and medium-sized producers are integrated into global value chains dominated by multinationals (García and Rofman, 2009), compelled to adopt the production and commercial practices dictated by agribusiness; others have become new employees offering agricultural services; and some have been directly displaced from their lands, leading them to migrate to urban areas.

Agribusiness represents a specific productive logic (Gras and Hernández, 2013) characterised by the implementation of 'modern' agroindustrial technologies. Originating from the Green Revolution, which aimed to increase productivity through greater mechanisation (thus reducing the need for human labour), the adoption of hybrid seeds, and intensive use of chemical inputs (e.g., fertilisers), agribusiness technology requires significant and sustained investment. This results in the concentration of capital in production processes and transforms countries and farmers into 'entities dependent on suppliers of inputs and equipment' (Rosset, 1998, p. 4).

The territorial development model of agribusiness is typically accompanied by increasing land hoarding through various forms such as leasing, contract farming, and land purchases (Gorenstein and Ortiz, 2016). While agribusinesses often focus on concentration of management rather than ownership (Hernández, 2009), in Argentina it has proliferated within a historically concentrated land tenure structure. Due to its inherent dynamics, agribusiness tends to displace small and medium-sized producers who cannot bear the rising costs associated with technological inputs (which require increasingly frequent applications of chemical inputs or the high rental costs driven by competition for land). Even landowners may find it more profitable to lease their land rather than engage in production themselves.

Land hoarding in Argentina has been accompanied by a process of foreignisation (Costantino, 2016). Between 1992–2001 and 2002–2013, not only did the average annual number of hectares acquired by foreigners increase (from 94,123 ha to 215,561 ha), but the average size of transactions also grew (from 32,114 ha to 61,912 ha). This increased foreign capital involvement is attributed to favourable international conditions, such as a sustained rise in raw material prices and low interest rates in large markets such as the United States, as well as state support for land purchases (59% of the total). According to the non-profit organisation GRAIN (2016), a similar trend occurred throughout South America: between 2006 and 2015, nearly

4 million hectares were acquired, with the investment sector predominantly composed of agribusiness and finance (93.1%), primarily aimed at producing soybeans (56.9%), corn (31%), and livestock (22.4%).

The concentration and foreignisation driven by agribusiness extend throughout the entire global value chain, reaching agrochemical marketing and commodity exports in Argentina. In 2016, three major companies—ChemChina-Syngenta, Bayer-Monsanto, and DowDupont—controlled 54.3% of the agrochemical market (Bertello, 2017). It is notable that these companies also lead the global seed market (Propato and Mercatante, 2019) and have a significant presence in Argentina. In the 2018/2019 export season, four foreign-owned companies accounted for 48% of the country's total external sales, with the top ten exporters making up 91% (Calzada et al., 2020). Moreover, just three commodities—soybeans, wheat, and corn—represented over 90% of exports.

This concentration on a few crops is further driven by the entry of financial capital into production. Gras and Hernández (2013) highlight that capital operates both 'from above' and 'from below'. On the one hand, speculation on international raw material prices leads to price increases and affects agribusiness production decisions and national productive specialisation. On the other hand, producers turn to financial instruments for insurance and financing through investment funds, which prioritise quick profits and result in privileging financial outcomes over productive ones (Gras and Hernández, 2013). Both logics intersect and create a favourable environment for commodity production. According to data from Indexmundi (n.d.), the international price of soybeans (Monsanto's RR, approved for use in Argentina in 1996) increased by 131.9% from December 1995 ($296) to August 2012 ($684), with notable peaks in 2004 and 2008. Meanwhile, Investing.com (n.d.) reports that the 10-year US bond rate, a key reference for investment decisions, fell by 72.2% (from 5.575% to 1.548%). The decline in the bond rate encourages capital investment, and the sustained rise in soybean prices (among other commodities) offers a secure destination for these investments.

The intensification of these extra-agrarian logics (Gras and Hernández, 2013), within the framework of a global food production regime, leads to a redefinition of why, how, and what is produced. This results in production that does not address local needs for food, job creation, or land as habitat. Instead, land becomes a mere commodity, stripped of its social and symbolic value.

As the agribusiness-driven territorial development model expands, nation-states are repositioned within global exploitation chains, internally reconfiguring their territories. For example, the growth in global market-oriented production (such as soybeans in Argentina since the 1990s) shifts internal borders. This occurs through the occupation of previously productive territories, the replacement of traditional productions, or the expansion of the agricultural frontier at the expense of traditional communities or native forests (Gras and Hernández, 2013, pp. 17–48). This expansion has various socio-environmental consequences, including biodiversity loss and health issues such as the poisoning of nearby communities. Thus, the incorporation of 'new' lands aids in capital valorisation and shifts the boundaries of dependency.

Where there is re-deterritorialisation, there is resistance

In response to the advance of agribusiness, counterhegemonic territorial development models have emerged, based on alternative modes of production that challenge the corporate food regime. These models aim to reconfigure territories to prioritise the reproduction of life and nature over capital accumulation, treating the market and capital as tools rather than objectives in themselves (Féliz, 2015).

Among the various approaches within alternative agriculture, agroecology has been embraced by international social movements like La Vía Campesina as a crucial component in building Food Sovereignty (La Vía Campesina, 2015, p. 1). It is seen as a form of resistance to an economic system that prioritises profit over life (La Vía Campesina, 2015, p. 2), a tool for struggle (Rosset and Martínez Torres, 2016), and a strategy to transform and establish local food production systems that are sovereign and resilient against the contingencies created by the current global system. In Argentina, popular peasant and indigenous organisations are also promoting agroecology nationwide and calling for state support (Foro Agrario, 2019).

Agroecology enables small producers, organisations, researchers, and technicians to remain engaged (Marasas et al. 2012). Its goal is to create productive agroecosystems that reduce reliance on external inputs, such as pesticides and energy, by fostering 'biological interactions and beneficial synergies between the components of the agroecosystem' (Altieri and Toledo, 2011, p. 5). This is achieved through practices like crop diversification, integration of crops with livestock, and the recovery and valorisation of traditional knowledge. Saquet (2021) highlights that agroecology is characterised by its promotion of 'peasant and local-based territorial development practices' (p. 100).

The significance of agroecology lies in its support for three forms of sovereignty: food, technology, and energy (Altieri and Toledo, 2011). Food sovereignty encompasses 'the right of people to nutritious and culturally appropriate food, produced sustainably and ecologically, and their right to determine their own food and production systems' (La Via Campesina, 2007, p. 1). By concentrating on local food production systems, driven by small-scale family farmers, peasants, and indigenous people, agroecology supports the expanded reproduction of both producers' and consumers' lives. To achieve food sovereignty, agroecology advocates for a dual break from the technologies inherited from the Green Revolution. First, it promotes ending reliance on agrochemicals, thereby breaking technological subordination. Second, it seeks to revalue local and ancestral knowledge, enabling small producers, family farmers, peasants, and indigenous people to move beyond the centralisation and legitimisation of modern agronomic knowledge. This shift empowers them to make their own decisions regarding production, marketing, and other aspects of their agricultural practices (Le Coq et al., 2017, p. 16). This dual rupture is part of a broader pursuit of technological sovereignty, which involves designing and managing agroecosystems according to agroecological principles. From this framework emerges the third form of sovereignty: energy sovereignty. This principle leverages local energy sources and plant biomass generated through production, providing a sustainable alternative to the fossil-fuel-dependent global food regime (Altieri and Toledo, 2011).

Rosset and Martínez Torres (2016) note that agroecology enhances the autonomy of those who adopt it, countering the dependency imposed by global exploitation chains. Although autonomy remains relative—since production must still circulate and be sold in local or nearby markets—its growing presence impacts multiple dimensions: productive (e.g., crop diversification), economic (e.g., reduced costs), social (e.g., reduced labour time), cultural (e.g., respect for the land), and environmental (e.g., ecological sustainability).

Agroecology facilitates the reterritorialisation of small producers, family farmers, peasants, and indigenous communities, challenging the dominant agribusiness logic. This reterritorialisation involves installing alternative logics and fostering supportive social relations for current and future generations, while promoting fair trade and respect for nature. For small producers, the territory becomes a 'shelter' for production and reproduction (Silveira, 2007), in contrast to agribusiness, where the territory is merely a 'platform for profit and a resource in its equation, rather than the condition of its existence' (Silveira, 2007, p. 23).

The territorial dispute between agroecology and agribusiness extends beyond material spaces into the realm of ideas and paradigms, each offering contrasting and opposing visions. Mançano Fernandes (2017) explains that immaterial territories are linked to 'the control and dominance over the knowledge construction process' (p. 29). Thought itself generates power relations, and as reterritorialisation processes are accompanied by differing conceptions, they also manifest in varied material realities. Toro-Mayorga and Dupuits (2021) argue that the co-production of knowledge—between grassroots social organisations and supportive actors such as the state—serves as a form of resistance. This co-production challenges the modernising ideal of achieving territorial development through technical notions of modernisation, efficiency, and professionalisation (Toro-Mayorga and Dupuits, 2021).

In this context, agroecology represents a foundation for developing territorial models that opposes the agribusiness paradigm. Agroecology is more than a set of practices or principles; it embodies 'a way of life' (La Vía Campesina, 2015, p. 3), with the territory serving as a fundamental pillar for its existence. Consequently, we argue that agroecology fosters the creation of territories centred on the expanded reproduction of life and the sustainability of nature. In doing so, it provides an alternative to the logic of agribusiness and the corporate food production regime, prioritising the production of healthy, sovereign food over the reproduction of capital.

Recent experiences in Argentina

As an example, we will describe instances in Argentina where agribusiness seeks to expand, alongside cases of resistance and the development of counterhegemonic territorial models.

The transgenic daily bread

On October 9, 2020, Argentina's Ministry of Agriculture, Livestock, and Fisheries issued Resolution No. 41/2020, authorising the commercialisation of IND-ØØ412-7 wheat. This is a transgenic wheat notable for its tolerance to drought and glufosinate-ammonium, a herbicide designed to replace glyphosate, which is currently used in some varieties of soybeans and corn.

A key in this wheat's approval was Brazil's commercial endorsement, as Brazil is the main international buyer of Argentine wheat. This endorsement, which came in November 2021, underscores Argentina's dependency on international markets, emphasising export capacity while neglecting the territorial impacts of introducing a new genetically modified organism (GMO). Historical experience with transgenic soybeans suggests that introducing a new transgenic crop typically results in increased agrochemical use (heightening technological dependence), greater pressure on the agricultural frontier (due to drought resistance), and consequently, more deforestation and displacement of family farmers, peasants, and indigenous people (Aranda, 2020). It also leads to increased business concentration along the supply chain, greater land pollution, and increased concerns over the effects on human health. This expansion deepens the territorialisation of agribusiness and the deterritorialisation of alternative agricultural practices. Additionally, the risk of cross-fertilisation—where GM wheat could contaminate other wheat varieties—raises concerns about the potential disappearance of non-GM varieties and the dominance of GM wheat.

The territorial dispute also plays out on an immaterial level. The potential contamination of traditional wheat varieties poses a significant challenge to food sovereignty. Wheat processing leads to flour, which is essential for bread and many staple foods in the Argentine diet. Allowing such GM wheat could undermine discussions about food production and consumption, impacting fundamental aspects of what we eat and how it is produced.

Mega pig farms against all odds

On July 6, 2020, the Ministry of Foreign Affairs, International Trade, and Cults announced a project in collaboration with the Ministry of Agriculture of China to boost Argentina's pork production by an additional 900,000 tons over four years (Ministry of Foreign Affairs, International Trade, and Worship Cults, 2020). While the specific details of the agreement are not publicly available, Argentine national news agency Télam (2020) reported that the plan involves establishing 25 farms, each with 12,000 sows, in various locations across the country. This initiative was funded by both Chinese and Argentine investments, with the primary goal of exporting pork to China, which has experienced a decline in its own production due to African swine fever (ASF).

The official rationale for this agreement is to add value to exports by producing pork domestically. Currently, Argentine soybeans, which are exported to China, are used to feed pigs. By producing pork within the country, Argentina aims to advance up the global value chain. However, this agribusiness venture, which applies the principles of the global food regime to livestock, brings additional pressure on the agricultural frontier. The large-scale and intensive nature of the proposed farms is expected to result in significant socio-environmental challenges, including overcrowding, excrement accumulation, soil and groundwater contamination, and excessive water use. In response to criticism, the Ministry has pledged to incorporate technology to mitigate environmental impacts.

In line with agribusiness principles, this agreement would lead to greater concentration, specialisation, and export focus, transforming territories into extractivist platforms despite socio-environmental costs. Jorge Neme, the Secretary of International Economic Relations, indicated that the farms will be situated in 'deserted areas' of the country, disregarding existing territories and communities, and reinforcing the agribusiness model in these regions (Barruti, 2020). Forcinito et al. (2021) argue that the project could displace small producers who focus on local and self-consumption and raise concerns about the quality of jobs created by these large-scale farms, which may be associated with higher risks of infectious diseases and occupational hazards.

Dependency is a central issue in this project. The production is tied to Chinese purchasing (trade dependence) and relies on the absence of disease outbreaks like ASF, as seen recently in Germany, where exports were halted due to an ASF outbreak. Additionally, technological dependence is evident, as China benefits from exporting production technology, which necessitates importing supplies and spare parts, and hiring technicians and workers from China. Ultimately, the agreement reinforces Argentina's role as a supplier in the corporate food regime.

In response, the National Forum for a Sovereign and Popular Agrarian Program (2020) proposed an alternative plan. This approach leverages the export opportunity but within an agroecological framework: establishing 1,000 to 1,500 smaller farms with 200 to 300 sows each, significantly reducing environmental risks associated with industrial production. Each farm would contribute to job creation, strengthen rural communities, and diversify production by incorporating agriculture. This proposal aims to (re)territorialise family, peasant, and indigenous agriculture, offering a counterhegemonic model to the industrial agribusiness approach.

Agroecological colonies for food sovereignty

The Union of Land Workers (UTT) is a national organisation comprising thousands of small-scale producers, both men and women, who aim to 'build another reality' (UTT, n.d.). The UTT gained significant public attention through its *verdurazos*—public fairs where vegetables are distributed or sold at affordable prices. These events serve to highlight the sector's challenges and advocate for public policies that support agroecology over the agribusiness model, which they argue makes farmers dependent on agrochemicals (Sotiru, 2021).

Amidst their demands for land and support for agroecology, the UTT envisioned creating agroecological urban supply colonies. In these colonies, groups of families would live and work together on the same property, producing food using agroecological methods. They would reduce costs by sharing production resources such as machinery and jointly addressing collective needs like health, education, and training (UTT, 2020). This model aims to provide families with secure land and decent work while offering nearby towns and cities access to healthy, local, and affordable food by cutting out intermediaries and reducing transportation costs. The approach emphasises respect for nature and the well-being of land, producers, neighbours, and consumers.

This vision began to materialise in 2015 with the establishment of the Agroecological Colony named 20 de Abril—Darío Santillán, followed by the creation of six more colonies across Buenos Aires, Entre Ríos, and Misiones. The UTT continues to negotiate with various levels of government to establish additional colonies. Acero Lagomarsino (2021) notes that reclaiming land for food production and housing has strengthened the UTT's union and political legitimacy within family farming.

Agroecological colonies demonstrate the potential of agroecology to (re) territorialise and build community networks, contrasting with the conventional industrial agriculture many farmers previously practised. As one producer observes, 'For many years, we were sold the idea that everything had to be healed with poison. Once you learn about agroecology, you spend much less money, and the vegetables are tastier and healthier' (UTT, 2020).

These colonies counter both real estate expansion—such as the case with the Agroecological Colony 28 de Noviembre in San Vicente, which is surrounded by private neighbourhoods—and monoculture expansion, like that of the Agroecological Colony of the Independent Producers of Puerto Piray, surrounded by pine monoculture plantations. Additionally, the colonies enhance autonomy by supplying food to nearby communities directly, ensuring the sale of production and reducing the need for long-distance food transportation. Direct marketing at fair prices is feasible because the land is owned by the producers, who can grow what their community consumes, as a producer from Puerto Piray, explains, 'direct marketing is possible because the land belongs to us, and we can grow what people consume' (UTT, 2020). Through these efforts, agroecological colonies centre on the expanded reproduction of life and nature, challenging the agribusiness and extractivist paradigms in practice.

Guaminí and the construction of a network to expand agroecology

The National Network of Municipalities and Communities that Promote Agroecology (RENAMA) comprises farmers, agricultural technicians, municipalities, government entities, academic and scientific organisations, and grassroots groups. Its goal is to facilitate the exchange of experiences and knowledge to transition towards agroecology within the agri-food system (RENAMA, n.d.). Despite its relatively recent establishment, RENAMA includes 30 municipalities in Argentina and one in Uruguay, involving 180 producers and covering 90,000 hectares.

RENAMA adopts agroecology as its conceptual framework for understanding and practicing agriculture, while also addressing the challenges posed by the current industrial agriculture model. The first municipality to join RENAMA was Guaminí in the Province of Buenos Aires. There, a group of eight producers, guided by agronomist Eduardo Cerdá, began with 100 hectares, seeking an alternative to agrochemical applications. By 2020, this area had expanded to 5,000 hectares (Jaroslavsky, 2020). The success of this initiative led the municipality to purchase a mill for processing agroecological wheat. The community mill now supplies whole wheat flour, free of pesticides, not only to Guaminí but also to nearby towns (Aranda, 2017). As interactions between Guaminí producers and those from other locations increased, RENAMA began to form, linking various agroecological experiences and enhancing collective knowledge and learning.

These extensive agroecology projects demonstrate the potential for developing territorial models that foster increasing autonomy from the detrimental practices of industrial agriculture and agribusiness. In Guaminí, for instance, producers have been able to (re)territorialise through agroecology, diversifying their production, reducing the use of fertilisers and agrochemicals, and obtaining their own seeds (Schwerdt and Cerdá, 2015). They have maintained their fields and homes and, collectively, advanced in the production of whole wheat flour. For the producers involved, the territorialisation of agroecology represents not only a shift in production methods but also a transformation in their practices, relationships with other producers and the state, and the values they uphold, including a commitment to biodiversity conservation. RENAMA's network operation helps to spread agroecological practices, amplifying resistance against agribusiness and serving as a counterweight to its expansion.

Conclusions

This work aims to contribute to the discussion on dependency, particularly its connection with territory, borders, and territorial development. We examine how the territorial transformations occurring in Latin America are deeply intertwined with dependency and the broad range of economic, social, health, ecological, political, and cultural consequences they entail. By focusing on commodity and food production in Argentina, we illustrate how dependency operates through territorial logics that facilitate the expanded valorisation and accumulation of capital. This expansion displaces internal borders and pressures new territories to adopt the agribusiness model. We specifically highlight two projects: the establishment of mega pig farms and the approval of a new transgenic wheat variety. These initiatives exemplify a territorial development model centred on capital reproduction, responding to the corporate food regime.

In contrast, we also present examples of resistance that embody counter-hegemonic development models, such as agroecology. These resistances focus on defending and building territories where the central values are the reproduction of life and nature, offering an alternative to the capital-driven advance and paving the way towards greater autonomy and sovereignty for Latin America.

Bibliography

Agrarian Forum. (2020, August). *About the Agreement with China for the industrial breeding of pigs for export*. National Forum for a Sovereign and Popular Agrarian Program. https://bit.ly/3jFQctU

Altieri, M.A., and Toledo, V.M. (2011). The agroecological revolution of Latin America: Rescuing nature, securing food sovereignty and empowering peasants (P. Alarcón-Chaires, Trans.), The Journal of Peasant Studies, 38(3), 587–612. https://bit.ly/37x7Udx

Aranda, D. (2017, May 9). Guaminí: The agroecological alternative. *The ink*. https://bit.ly/3xJMtRe

Aranda, D. (Ed.). (2020). Atlas of transgenic agribusiness in the Southern Cone: Monocultures, resistance and proposals of the people (Action for Biodiversity). *Action for Biodiversity*. https://bit.ly/3oOdtgH

Barruti, S. (2020, September 15). The pig war: The agreement between Argentina and China. *Cow*. https://bit.ly/3AA2A5C

Bell, P., and Cleaver, H. (1982). Marx's Crisis Theory as a Theory of Class Struggle, *Research in Political Economy*, 5(5), 189–261.

Bertello, F. (2017, June 26). Winners and losers of the agrochemical market [Daily]. *The nation*. https://bit.ly/3iyDgGR

Blanco, J. (2010). Espacio y Territorio: Elementos teórico-conceptuales implicados en el análisis geográfico. En M.V. Fernández Caso y R. Gurevich (Eds.), *Geografía. Nuevos temas, nuevas preguntas. Un temario para su enseñanza*. Biblos.

Caffentzis, G. (2013). *In letters of blood and fire: Work, machines, and the crisis of capitalism*. PM Press: Common Notions. https://bit.ly/3s6dw82

Calzada, J., Bergero, P., and Terré, E. (2020). Ranking of agro-export companies according to sales of the 2018/19 commercial campaign. *Rosario Stock Exchange [Weekly News - Markets]*. https://bit.ly/3CBk82Z

Castells, M. (2009). *Communication and power*. In: M. Hernandez, Trans. First ed. Ed. Alianza. https://www.felsemiotica.com/descargas/Castells-Manuel-Comunicaci%C3%B3n-y-poder.pdf

Costantino, A. (2016). Foreign capital and land grabbing: Social conflicts and accumulation through dispossession in Argentina, *Journal of Social Studies*, 35(55), 137–149. https://bit.ly/3GROfnJ

Entrena Durán, F. (2010). Dynamics of local territories in the present circumstances of globalization, *Sociological Studies*, XXVIII(84), 691–728. https://bit.ly/3oOdGAv

Federici, S. (2018). The patriarchy of the salary. Feminist criticisms of Marxism. *Dream Traffickers – Maps*. https://bit.ly/3jOa2Dc
Féliz, M. (2015). What to do… With development? Neodevelopment, good living and popular alternatives, *Society and Economy*, 28, 29–49. https://bit.ly/33qgEUn
Forcinito, K., Glosa Zuazua, N., Varela, P., and Rodríguez Enríquez, C. (2021). *Argentina at the crossroads: From Chinese foreign investment in mega-pig farms to just ecological transition policies* (Situation Analysis Series No. 28). Interdisciplinary Center for the study of public policies. https://bit.ly/3gOlopE
Foro Agrario. (2019). Primeras conclusiones. *Foro Nacional por un Programa Agrario Soberano y Popular*. https://bit.ly/2VO72hK
García, A., and Rofman, A. (2009). Agribusiness and fragmentation in Argentine agriculture: From marginalization towards an alternative proposal, *Agrarian World, Journal of Rural Studies*, No. 18, Center for Rural Historical Studies, Faculty of Humanities and Educational Sciences, UNLP. https://bit.ly/3k1Mz1N
García Guerreiro, L. and Wahren, J. (2014). Campesinado, territorios en disputa y nuevas estrategias de comercialización de la producción campesina en la Argentina. In: Veredas. *Revista del pensamiento sociológico N°. 28 / Año 15* (pp. 297–342). México: Universidad Autónoma de México-Xochimilco.
Gorenstein, S., and Ortiz, R. (2016). The land in dispute. Agriculture, accumulation and territory in recent Argentina, *ReLaER, Latin American Journal of Rural Studies*, I(2), 1–26. https://bit.ly/3yQAQcc
GRAIN. (2016). The global farmland grab in 2016: how big, how bad? Available at GRAIN | The global farmland grab in 2016: how big, how bad? (last accessed 28.11.2024).
Gras, C., and Hernández, V.A. (2013). The pillars of the agribusiness model and its business styles. In C. Gras and V.A. Hernández (Eds.), *Agriculture as a business: Production, society and territories in globalization* (pp. 17–48). Byblos Publishing House.
Haesbaert, R. (2011). *The myth of deterritorialization: From the "end of territories" to multiterritoriality*. XXI Century Editorial.
Harvey, D. (2005). *The new imperialism: Accumulation by dispossession*. CLACSO. https://bit.ly/2VO2Ij9
Hernandez, V.A. (2009). Globalized rurality and the agribusiness paradigm in the American pampas. In C. Gras and V.A. Hernández (Eds.), *Rural Argentina: From family farming to agribusiness* (pp. 39–64). First edition. Byblos Publishing House.
Indexmundi. (s.f.). (n.d.). Soybeans—Daily Price—Commodity Prices. *Indexmundi*. Retrieved August 11, 2021, from https://bit.ly/3GThjLF
Investing.com. (s.f.). (n.d.). Historical data of the United States 10-year bond. *Investing.com*. Retrieved August 11, 2021, from https://bit.ly/3gRSJQB
Jaroslavsky, M. (2020, October 31). *Guaminí: 5000 hectares of agroecology*. Tierra Viva News Agency. https://bit.ly/3lYo7Rh
La Via Campesina. (2007). *Nyéléni Declaration. (Nyéléni, Sélingué, Mali)*. Via Campesina Spanish. https://bit.ly/3v0V0S5
La Vía Campesina. (2015). Declaración del Foro Internacional sobre Agroecología. *Via Campesina Español*. https://bit.ly/3BpyW4w
Lagomarsino Steel, P. (2021). Socio-spatial strategies of peri-urban family farming: The case of the Land Workers Union in the RMBA, *Rural Studies*, 11(21). https://bit.ly/34DX7Ax
Le Coq, J.-F., Sachet, E., Vazquez, L., Schmitt, C., and Sabourin, E. (2017). Agroecology concepts and analytical framework. In E. Sabourin, M.M. Patrol, J.-F. Le Coq, L. Vazquez, and P.A. Niederle (Eds.), *Public policies in favor of agroecology in Latin America and The Caribbean*. Evangraf/Human Breeding, PP-AL-FAO Network.

Llanos-Hernández, L. (2010). El concepto del territorio y la investigación en las ciencias sociales. *Agricultura, sociedad y desarrollo*, 7(3), 207–220. https://bit.ly/3sNjNWJ
Luxemburg, R. (2018). *The accumulation of capital. Germinal – in defense of Marxism*. Sedov International Editions. Germinal. https://bit.ly/3jJxO3s
Madoery, O. (2013). Three theses for a political re-interpretation of development. *Topics and Debates*, 26, 13–37. https://bit.ly/3s8Oq8j
Mançano Fernandes, B. (2011). Territories, theory and politics. In: G. Calderón and E. León (Coord.), *Discovering social spatiality in Latin America. Collection "How to think about geography"* (Vol. 3). Itaca Publishing House. https://bit.ly/3jJWOHM
Mançano Fernandes, B. (2017). Territories and Food Sovereignty. *ReLaER, Latin American Journal of Rural Studies*, II(3).
Manzanal, M. (2007). Territory, Power and Institutions. A critical perspective. In: M. Manzanal, M. Archers, and B. Nussbaumer (comp.), *Territories in Construction, Actors, plots and governments, between cooperation and conflict* (pp. 15–50). CICCUS. http://www.scba.gov.ar/includes/descarga.asp?id=21382&n=Territorio-poder-e-instituciones.Mabel-Manzanal.pdf
Manzanal, M. (2014). Development. A critical perspective from the analysis of power and territory, *Economía Magazine*, 283, 17–48. https://bit.ly/3sfH7vJ
Manzanal, M. (2017). Territory, Power and Sojization in the Latin American Southern Cone, *The Argentine case, Agrarian World*, 18(37), 048. https://bit.ly/3JyyV1a
Marasas M., De Luca L.C., Ullé J.A. 2012. *El camino de la transición agroecológica*. Buenos Aires: Ediciones INTA.
Marini, R.M. (2015). Dialectic of dependency (1973). In: C.E. Martins (Ed.), *Latin America, dependence and globalization/Ruy Mauro Marin* (pp. 107–150). XXI Century Editors/CLACSO.
Martínez Godoy, D., and Clark, P. (2015). Territorial development in Ecuador: Conceptual and conjunctural elements for the analysis of local perspectives in times of globalization. In: D. Martínez Godoy and P. Clark (Eds.), *Territorial development in Ecuador: Current situation and perspectives* (pp. 15–36). First edition. Abya Yala. https://bit.ly/33oz1ZF
McMichael, P. (2006). Global Development and The Corporate Food Regime. In: *Research in Rural Sociology and Development* (Vol. 11, pp. 265–299). Emerald (MCB UP). https://bit.ly/3LEgQjT
Ministry of Foreign Affairs, International Trade and Worship. (2020, July 6). *Interview between Foreign Minister Felipe Solá and the Minister of Commerce of the People's Republic of China Zhong Shan*. Argentina: Ministry of Foreign Affairs, International Trade and Worship. https://bit.ly/3jIe7ZL
Ortiz, R. (1998). *Another Territory: Essays on the Contemporary World*. Andrés Bello Agreement.
Patel, R., and Moore, J.W. (2017). *A History of the World in Seven Cheap Things: A Guide to Capitalism, Nature, and the Future of the Planet*. University of California Press.
Propato, P., and Mercatante, E. (2019). *The global and national seed market. The concentration on seed production and its effects*. National Seed Institute (INASE), Ministry of Agriculture, Fisheries and Livestock. https://bit.ly/37Oh9Gt
RENAMA. (s.f.). (n.d.). RENAMA – National Network of Municipalities and Communities that promote Agroecology – Argentina – For Health, the Countryside and Life. Retrieved January 21, 2021, from http://www.renama.org/
Rosset, P.M. (1998). The Crisis of Conventional Agriculture, Input Substitution, and the Agroecological Approach. *Food Firsts*, 17. https://bit.ly/37zCoeS
Rosset, P.M., and Martínez Torres, M.E. (2016). Agroecology, territory, repeasantization and social movements. *Social studies, Journal of Scientific Research*, 25(47), 275–299. https://bit.ly/37zCoLU

Saquet, M.A. (2021). *Consciousness of class and place, praxis and territorial development*. First edition. CLACSO. https://bit.ly/368k9zA

Schneider, S., and Peyré Tartagua, I.G. (2006). Territory and territorial approach, from cognitive references to contributions applied to the analysis of rural social processes. In M. Manzanal, G. Neiman, and M. Lattuada (Eds.), *Rural Development. Organizations, Institutions and Territory* (pp. 71–102). CICCUS. https://bit.ly/3HTKwYg

Schwerdt, M.G., and Cerdá, E. (2015, October 7–9). *Development of the first experiences in extensive agroecological crops promoted by the municipal state in Guaminí, province of Buenos Aires*. La Plata: V Latin American Congress of Agroecology - SOCLA. https://bit.ly/3LHxbEL

Silveira, M.L. (2007). The corporate territories of globalization, *Geography*, 3(3), 13–26. https://bit.ly/3gRQU6o

Sotiru, M.N. (2021). Union of Land Workers: "We have been doing food sovereignty exercises, preparing for this society that we are building". In: D. Melón and M. Relli Ugartamendía (Eds.), *Geographies of conflict: Civilization crisis, resistance and popular constructions in the capitalist periphery* (pp. 77–82). First edition. https://bit.ly/3oVholq

Telam. (2020, August 4). *The agreement with China to produce pork provides for an investment of US$3.8 billion*. Telam. https://bit.ly/3CBtlbz

Toro-Mayorga, L., and Dupuits, E. (2021). Coproducing territorial development: Public-community strategies for water and food in Imbabura-Ecuador. *Eutopia, Journal of Territorial Economic Development*, 19, 157–174. https://bit.ly/3LDQfnd

UTT. (2020, December 26). *Agroecological Colonies: A proposal that is growing throughout the country*. Union of Land Workers. https://bit.ly/3xEf3Dx

UTT. (s.f.). (n.d.). *About us*. Union of Land Workers. Retrieved January 20, 2021, from https://bit.ly/3rT9OA4

6 Yerba mate

Technoscientific political arena and territorial development in the Iguaçu Valley (Paraná, southern Brazil)

Ricardo Gomes Luiz and Maclovia Corrêa da Silva

Introduction

Yerba mate (*Ilex paraguariensis*) is a plant native to South America used in the preparation of beverages that are widely consumed today. It is highly commercialized in a market with growth potential. One of the main producing regions is the Iguaçu Valley, southern Brazil. The Iguaçu Valley is a rural area comprising ten municipalities in southern Paraná, with a population of 200,000 and an economy strongly based on agriculture. According to the 2017 Brazilian agricultural census, there are 14,523 rural properties, 78% of which (11,336) are small-scale and family-run. Yerba mate is cultivated in 3,900 family agricultural production units (IBGE, 2019).

Most yerba mate producers are family farmers, whose work generates social, economic, and environmental benefits. However, in this economic activity, there is a technoscientific political arena in which family farmers do not participate. The region is notable for its significant yerba mate production, involving family farmers in the productive chain and featuring relevant cultural and environmental characteristics. The technical and technological aspects of yerba mate cultivation are significant, given the debates around traditional systems and practices aimed at increasing productivity. Within this context, this chapter addresses the following research question: How do technoscientific narratives influence yerba mate farming and its role in the territorial development of the Iguaçu Valley?

Productive activities in rural territories receive technical and technological instructions that restrict choices and pressure farmers to adjust their practices. These adjustments are related to the integration of rural production into the market, in which low price is one of the imperatives for the products offered. To produce more and at reduced costs, agricultural activities are guided to employ technologies that enable increased productivity. This allows for the supply of cheaper products and favours agreements and their commercialization. This chapter aims at analysing this political arena from a technoscientific perspective in the territory of Iguaçu Valley, through a selection and analysis of the literature on technoscience, political arena, territory, and development.

DOI: 10.4324/9781032650241-8

The methodology included a selection of technical documents and events that influence yerba mate cultivation. The results show that territorial development is influenced by scientific and technological narratives that are not necessarily connected to the characteristics of the territory. Moreover, we show the conformation of a political arena that invades the circuits that determine the destinations of the modes of production, as well as which actors are included or excluded from the configuration of this arena.

Technology, technoscience, and development

New technologies provide guidance in the fields of seeds, plant variety, equipment, inputs, management, and harvest, as well as in the daily lives of people in the territories. However, they also create situations of dependence. Bazzo et al. (2003) classify this phenomenon as technological essentialism, that is, the belief that technology alone promotes well-being and a better life. This dependence corresponds to technological determinism, outlined by Feenberg, with the argument that technologies have an autonomous functional logic, causing society to move towards the pursuit of modernity, and consequently become dependent on a non-social dimension that acts in the social environment (Feenberg, 2010, p. 72). There is a delineation of capitalism for technoscientific action, or technology as the organizer of the contemporary world, highlighting capitalist characteristics where speed and efficiency are put at the service of the imperative of profit maximisation (Dias, 2021, p. 56).

Dagnino (2019), however, shows that these notions of well-being and modernity are myths and create social exclusion because they are both constituted in contexts of social asymmetries that impede the collective use and distribution of technological benefits. As Dias (2011) argues, this creates a restrictive environment that includes similar views and repels differing ones, shaping scientific and technological policy formation. These processes also unfold in public discussions of technical ideas and propositions.

In Latin America, the specifics of scientific and technological policies are historically linked to promoting development, aiming to emulate the trajectories of more capitalist-integrated, 'developed' nations. This developmental focus emphasises the importance of science and technology without addressing social differences between the countries and regions. Furthermore, the triumphalist view of technoscience can obscure conflicts between dominant classes in the political arena and those excluded from it (Dias, 2011). Technoscientific political action as sociotechnical ordering holds power beyond productive activities (Dias, 2021). In Latin America, technoscientific approaches influence territorial formation, often failing to integrate diverse actors and productive activities. It also requires state alignment and support, resulting in a unidimensional manifestation of development (Raffestin, 1993).

This limits the social, material, technical, and economic relations that shape human action and form the territory (Raffestin, 1993).

The relationship between technoscience and development in Latin America often fails to consider the territories and the actors directly involved. As technoscientific changes take place, there is a risk of eroding the bonds that shape territorial identity and the territory itself. Escobar (2011) warns against development models that overlook or seek to replace local environmental, cultural, and economic realities. Instead, he advocates for development models that are aligned with local realities, supported by cognitive justice and constitutive relationality (Escobar, 2014). Saquet (2017) complements this idea by emphasising the political action of territorial actors who can create a non-hegemonic paradigm, forming a counter-movement to external forces that dictate development without local ties. He highlights the immaterial aspects of the territorial approach, where territory construction occurs through the actions of actors who associate based on specificities, differences, and equalities, in a dynamic of continuities and discontinuities (Saquet, 2020).

Based on the above, this research's analytical framework was based on three categories of analysis:

1. Technological triumphalism: This category includes concepts such as the centrality and essentialism of technology (Bazzo et al., 2003), technological determinism (Feenberg, 2010), and the myths of technology that can lead to social exclusion (Dagnino, 2019).
2. Performance of the technoscientific political arena: Concepts in this category focus on technoscience associated with capitalist attributes and sociotechnical ordering (Dias, 2021), and the role of technology in shaping political arenas (Dias, 2011).
3. The technoscientific political arena and territorial development: This category examines how technoscience reduces relational characteristics in territory formation (Raffestin, 1993), contributes to territorial development that may ignore local realities (Escobar, 2011), and supports development models based on cognitive justice and relationality (Escobar, 2014). It also includes perspectives on the political action of territorial actors (Saquet, 2017) and the immaterial aspects of territory (Saquet, 2020).

Table 6.1 outlines the analytical framework, detailing each category and its theoretical basis.

These analytical categories work together to examine how the political actions of technoscience influence and impact the territory. The central theme across these categories is that technology often becomes deterministic, influences political actions, limits the participation of those aligned with technological and scientific interests, and ultimately affects the territory.

Table 6.1 Categories of analysis and theoretical basis

Category of Analysis	*Theoretical Basis*
Technological Triumphalism	For farmers, technology imposes restrictive instructions that limit their ability to adapt practices, disregarding diversity and traditional methods. This creates a context where technology is central and essentialist, defining human activity (Bazzo et al., 2003). It reflects technological determinism, which focuses on productivity gains at the expense of natural and social systems, making society increasingly dependent on technology and the modernity it promises (Feenberg, 2010). However, the supposed benefits of technology—such as well-being and modernity—are often myths that lead to social exclusion. This is because access to technology is often restricted by financial barriers, privileges, and demands for abandoning traditions and altering social structures (Dagnino, 2019).
Performance of the Technoscientific Political Arena	Technology's influence on production intertwines with scientific knowledge, creating technoscience driven by capitalist goals like productivity, speed, and efficiency for profit maximisation (Dias, 2021). Technoscience shapes sociotechnical ordering, impacting and altering territorial formation (Dias, 2021). The power of technology manifests in productivity-focused scientific discourse, which forms a political arena where technoscientific policies and actions are defined. Within this arena, dominant classes leverage technoscience to obscure conflicts and exclude those seeking to maintain their autonomy (Dias, 2011).
The Technoscientific Political Arena and Territorial Development	Technoscience diminishes relational aspects in territorial formation, affecting both unidimensional and multidimensional scales (Raffestin, 1993). It often ignores and seeks to replace local realities (Escobar, 2011). Escobar (2014) advocates for development models based on cognitive justice and relationality. Saquet emphasises the need for territorial actors to adopt a political perspective to resist external forces shaping development and to foster the territory's unique qualities and dynamics (Saquet, 2017; Saquet, 2020).

Methodology

The methodology, based on qualitative methods, consisted of four stages. The first stage involved describing yerba mate cultivation systems in the Iguaçu Valley. The second stage focused on constructing an analytical framework, using concepts from the literature review to form analytical categories. These concepts helped understand the aspects of a scientific and technological political arena, demonstrating this sphere as a field of decision-making that influences various realities. The study measured the technoscientific implications of the political arena on territorial development. To complete the analytical framework, the meaning of development in relation to the aspects that form the territory and territorialities was discussed. The selection of Latin American researchers was integral to the literature review due to their deep understanding of the particularities and dynamics of the region.

The third stage involved selecting and analysing four documents and events that illustrate the functioning of the technoscientific political arena, as well as the dominant narratives across technoscientific approaches to yerba mater cultivation. These included a technical publication (Penteado Junior & Goulart, 2019) from the Brazilian Agricultural Research Corporation (Embrapa), a key Brazilian public institution in agricultural research; the programme content of two public technoscientific events on yerba mate production, one organized by Embrapa (Embrapa Florestas, 2020) and the other by the Federal Institute of Santa Catarina (IFSC) (Instituto Federal de Santa Catarina, 2020); and three public hearing sessions on a proposed bill to regulate the management of Araucaria Forest areas in Paraná, which could be associated with yerba mate cultivation areas (Assembleia Legislativa do Estado do Paraná, 2019).

The fourth stage consisted of analysing these experiences using the constructed analytical framework, to identify dominant narratives. This analysis focused on the narratives and actors who promote them. These actors were divided between family farmers and technicians and specialists. The study examined how these actors' agency, driven by the technoscientific discourse, seeks to guide yerba mate cultivation through technoscientific narratives, excluding other possibilities of alternative engagement. It showed how the actors' agency creates an environment where the technoscientific discourse prevails and favours productivity in the name of territorial development.

In this way, the study met its objective of analysing this case study as a scientific and technological political arena that, with development intentions, impacts the Iguaçu Valley territory. The analyses aimed to verify the argument that scientific and technological policies and actions influence territorial development without necessarily aligning with the territory's environmental, social, and economic characteristics.

Yerba mate cultivation in the Iguaçu Valley

The study focused on yerba mate cultivation systems in southern Brazil, an economic activity based on the cultivation of *Ilex paraguariensis*, native to the ecosystems of Brazil, Paraguay, and Argentina (Oliveira & Rotta, 1985).

Yerba mate leaves are used in their natural form or dehydrated as extract and essence for products such as food, cosmetics, and pharmaceuticals (Mazuchowski & Rucker, 1997). However, yerba mate is primarily used to prepare beverages widely consumed in southern South America and, to a lesser extent, in other parts of the world.

Yerba mate's economic activity forms an international trade valued at USD 1.5 billion in 2020, projected to exceed USD 2 billion by 2027 (360 Research Reports, 2020). Annual production was 1.78 million tons in 2018, distributed among Argentina (809.3 thousand tons), Brazil (856.9 thousand tons), and Paraguay (116.2 thousand tons) (Dirección General de Estadística Encuestas y Censos, 2020; IBGE, 2020a, 2020b; Instituto Nacional de la Yerba Mate, 2021).

In Brazil, yerba mate is primarily cultivated by family farmers using two main methods: full sun monocultures and shaded agroforestry systems, which integrate existing vegetation (Chaimsohn & Souza, 2012; Embrapa Florestas, 2017; Marques, 2014). Shaded cultivation offers unique environmental benefits, contributing to the maintenance of the threatened Araucaria Forest. It also preserves cultural heritage of indigenous peoples who domesticated the plant and developed techniques for its preparation and consumption. Additionally, the experiences of colonizers have influenced the development of these cultivation systems (Gerhardt, 2013; Luiz, 2017; Marques, 2014; Nimmo et al., 2020; Nogueira, 2021). Currently, these characteristics continue to generate knowledge, techniques, and the pursuit of autonomy, contributing to local development.

In the Iguaçu Valley region, the yerba mate economy connects with the traditions of shaded systems and the high productivity possibilities proposed by technoscience. In 2019, about 40% of Brazilian production (346.400.000 tons) came from the Iguaçu Valley, with a production value of BRL 367 million (USD 97.5 million) (IBGE, 2019, 2020a, 2020b). To support agricultural production, yerba mate cultivation systems in the Iguaçu Valley involve actors from diverse areas who dialogue and influence the production chain. Table 6.2 presents the composition of these actors and their roles in yerba mate cultivation systems.

The composition of this set of actors is important for understanding the continuity of the analyses carried out, as will be developed in the next section.

Results and discussion

When analysing yerba mate cultivation in the Iguaçu Valley, it becomes clear that technoscientific efforts are driven by productivism principles. This focus on maximising production and sales reflects principles of modernity and development used to achieve these goals. However, too much focus on technoscience has brought unintended consequences, such as excluding farmers from decision-making, disregarding traditional production methods, and ignoring the cultural and territorial diversity inherent in agricultural practices.

In the study's third methodological stage, four technical documents and events were chosen for analysis. These initiatives are relevant due to the

Table 6.2 Actors of yerba mate cultivation systems in the Iguaçu Valley

Actor	*Description*
Farmers	These are the farmers who cultivate yerba mate on their rural properties, most of which are family-scale and average 20 hectares. Besides yerba mate, they grow other crops and raise livestock. Their activities are linked to the preservation of native vegetation in threatened ecosystems of southern Brazil. In yerba mate cultivation, their work includes establishing plantations, managing crops, and pruning branches for leaf extraction, which are then sent to industries for processing.
Yerba Mate Companies	These companies buy yerba mate leaves from farmers for processing into beverage ingredients. In the Iguaçu Valley, there are about 40 yerba mate companies, most of which are small in terms of capacity, processing, and revenue. These companies vary in their involvement with the production chain: some control the entire process from leaf acquisition to packaging and sales, others handle only parts of the process, and some focus solely on export. Larger companies may also develop their own farms and provide technical assistance to farmers.
Government (Executive Branch)	These are government agencies that design public policies and regulations. In the past, they significantly influenced the yerba mate economy through price policies and commercial regulation. Currently, they focus more on technical assistance, extension actions, and compliance inspections covering environmental, social, economic, and sanitary aspects of agricultural production. These agencies also collect and process agricultural data and statistics. In Brazil, the Executive Branch operates at federal, state, and municipal levels.
Legislators	They have the public function and authority to propose laws for consideration by the Executive Branch. Recently, they have shown interest in debating legislation and regulatory adjustments to support the yerba mate production chain.
Researchers	Professionals who work in public agricultural research and development organisations like Embrapa. They focus on yerba mate management techniques, including plantation establishment, growth management, pruning, and genetic selection and improvement. Their research often involves collaboration with private companies and other research institutions such as universities, and can also be contracted by companies to develop exclusive cultivars.
Extensionists	Technical professionals, primarily from public companies, who provide assistance and guidance for managing yerba mate plantations and rural properties. Extensionists apply scientific research developments in the field, helping farmers implement improved practices.

region's significance in the yerba mate economy and its impact on both national and international markets. Table 6.3 outlines these selected documents and events. Notably, however, none of these are formal public policies or government programmes, at least yet. While there are laws like the National Yerba Mate Policy (Brasil, 2019) and the State Policy for Yerba Mate Incentive in Paraná (Paraná, 2018), they lack concrete regulations, funding, and administrative actions needed for practical implementation, such as enforcement and penalties for violations. The language in these laws often uses vague terms like support, promote, and encourage but does not specify actionable steps. This gap in policy effectiveness highlights the dependence on technoscience to address productivity challenges that government policies fail to resolve.

Table 6.3 Analysed documents and events

Document/Event		*Description*
1	Erva 20: Production system for yerba mate (Penteado Junior & Goulart, 2019)	Technical publication providing operational instructions for establishing and maintaining yerba mate plantations. It aims to increase productivity by targeting a yield of 20 tons of yerba mate leaves per hectare per year, compared to the average 8 tons per hectare typically achieved in shaded cultivations.
2	Public hearings (2019–2020) on proposed bill 537/2019, which 'establishes rules for protection, sustainable management, and compensation instruments for the preservation of the Araucaria Forest' (Assembleia Legislativa do Estado do Paraná, 2019)	Bill aimed at regulating management practices that balance the conservation of native Mixed Ombrophilous Forest (Araucaria Forest) with agricultural production, particularly through the cultivation of native species like yerba mate.
3	Webinar Araucária e Erva-mate (Instituto Federal de Santa Catarina, 2020)	Event featuring a series of technical presentations on yerba mate production, organized by the Federal Institute of Santa Catarina, a higher education institution. The event was held virtually over five sessions from July to August 2020.
4	Erva-mate XXI: Innovation and Technologies for the Yerba Mate Sector (Embrapa Florestas, 2020)	Virtual event organised by Embrapa. It was a series of technical lectures about yerba mate production systems, knowledge transfer, research dissemination, innovations, technologies, and public policies. The event included five panels held from October to December 2020.

The association between the examined documents and events, and the analytical categories highlight the role of technoscience in shaping the former, as we will explain in the following section.

Technological triumphalism

The publication Erva 20 (1) and the technical lectures from the events Webinar (3) and Erva-mate XXI (4) provide detailed instructions for implementing yerba mate plantations and improving the performance of yerba mate trees. These instructions aim to increase productivity, standardise plant characteristics, and ensure that the final product meets market preferences.

To achieve these goals, the recommendations include, first, homogenizing plantations and encouraging uniformity to enhance productivity, as the existing heterogeneity in diversified rural properties is seen as inefficient; second, acquiring improved cultivars, prioritising those developed through field and lab research that promise higher yields per hectare and meet market standards. These instructions serve as a practical guide to address the gaps left by volatile government policies, providing clear methods for achieving higher productivity. However, the focus on increasing production and market access overlooks biodiversity conservation and landscape changes.

This technoscientific approach reflects the triumphalist view of technology, which prioritises productivity over traditional cultivation methods and inherited knowledge. This emphasis aligns with the essentialist and deterministic perspective of technology (Bazzo et al., 2003; Feenberg, 2010), which advocates replacing diverse production methods with standardised, technologically advanced practices. Besides, while these technologies promise modernity and efficiency, they may not be accessible to all farmers. Cultivars developed by private companies can create barriers, as not all farmers can afford them. This limitation can turn the promise of technological benefits into a process of exclusion (Dagnino, 2019).

Performance of the technoscientific political arena

In the three technical events analysed (2, 3, and 4), technology and scientific research results in technoscience specifically tailored to yerba mate cultivation systems. This technoscience is closely aligned with capitalist practices, such as the hiring of researchers from public institutions by private companies (Dias, 2021). While the legality of this practice is not in question, it highlights the restrictive nature of the technoscientific political arena (Dias, 2011), where family farmers' participation and representation are limited. The Erva-mate XXI (4) event is an exception, featuring three initiatives aimed at benefiting farmers among its 20 presentations. Nonetheless, the dominant role of technoscientific actors created an imbalance of power.

Public hearings on the proposed bill by the Paraná legislative assembly (2) excluded farmers from discussions. Typically, only those with research backgrounds or market expertise are typically given a platform. As a result, farmers' perspectives are rarely heard, leading to potential disconnects between policy and the realities of yerba mate cultivation. Similarly, extension services provided by the government, as showcased in the Erva-mate XXI event (4), reflect techniques from more commercially focused crops, promoting simplification and standardisation in yerba mate cultivation.

The persistence of this technoscientific agenda aligns with the concept of sociotechnical ordering, which imposes actions and frameworks on farmers, favouring large-scale agricultural practices over small-scale methods (Dias, 2021). Consequently, family farmers lose agency to the centralised power of technoscientific decision-makers.

Technoscientific political arena and territorial development

Developmental intentions are not explicitly stated in any of the documents and events analysed. However, the public hearings for the bill frequently emphasise the pursuit of development, and the technoscientific triumphalism reflects a strong emphasis on development as modernity, evident for two main reasons: first, the impact of these initiatives on various aspects of territorial development—economic, social, cultural, and environmental; second, the lack of discussion on development in public hearing discourses, which is often equated and limited to economic growth. Indeed, the triumphalist nature of technoscience focuses on a narrow, unidimensional approach to development, as described by Raffestin (1993). In the case analysed here, technoscience imposes a single-directional relationship with farmers, leaving little room for diverse opinions or proposals. It overlooks the nuanced exchanges that contribute to forming the territory.

Technoscience often dismisses local realities and landscapes (Escobar, 2011). This marginalises the historical and cultural practices of farmers, effectively negating development models that emphasise cognitive justice and relationality (Escobar, 2014). Consequently, the development potential seen in these experiences overlooks the social and environmental benefits of yerba mate cultivation in the Iguaçu Valley. Similarly, the territorial values highlighted by Saquet (2017, 2020) are not realised. Technoscience's essentialist approach limits the political agency of territorial subjects (Saquet, 2017), excluding farmers from the technoscientific sphere. This exclusion prevents them from challenging external forces that shape development directions (Saquet, 2017) and diminishes the immaterial aspects of the territory (Saquet, 2020). Practices integral to farmers' lives—such as shaded yerba mate cultivation techniques—embody historical knowledge, cultural traditions, and ecosystem stewardship. These practices contribute to ecosystem services, support native vegetation, and maintain the relationship between farmers and their environment, which is not adequately recognised or valued in technoscientific frameworks.

Conclusions

Through the study of yerba mate cultivation and the narratives of four documents/events, this chapter highlights a generalised historical perspective of development, which often combines technology and science to boost economic activities. In Latin America, this approach is prevalent, with technoscience playing a key role in strategies aimed at improving international commercial positioning, increasing financial resources, and distributing income. However, technoscience's triumphalism tends to be deterministic, imposing capitalist goals of profit maximisation and productivity, which can lead to social, cultural, and environmental erosion in territorial development.

Academia in Latin America reflects this reality, as demonstrated by the authors whose works were used to construct the analytical categories. Their research is deeply rooted in Latin American contexts, producing knowledge that bridges global concepts with local realities. These scholars criticise academic hegemony while advocating for recognition of alternative ways of living in Latin America. This includes researchers focused on technoscience, technological determinism, and development models, as well as those reflecting on territoriality. The chapter's contribution lies in synthesising these diverse ideas to provide new insights into technoscientific perspectives on territorial development.

Applying concepts of technoscience, political arena, and territorial development to yerba mate cultivation reveals a disconnection between technological advances and local realities. This means that while farmers continue to produce yerba mate, they are excluded from the technoscientific political arena, neglecting their engagement in developmental proposals. Despite this, the immaterial aspects of the territory remain integral to their practices. The narratives analysed illustrate how technoscientific actors influence rural development standards. These actors are focused on economic success through market integration and productivity. However, there was limited scope for sociotechnical adjustments that could better align with local needs and resources.

Bibliography

360 Research Reports. (2020). Global Yerba Mate Market Research Report 2020. https://www.360researchreports.com/global-yerba-mate-market-15063705

Assembleia Legislativa do Estado do Paraná. (2019). Projeto de Lei 537/2019. http://portal.assembleia.pr.leg.br/index.php/pesquisa-legislativa/proposicao?idProposicao=85190

Bazzo, W.A., Linsingen, I.V., and Pereira, L.T. do V. (2003). Introdução aos estudos CTS (Ciência, Tecnologia e Sociedade). Organização dos Estados Ibero-americanos para a Educação, a Ciência e a Cultura (OEI). http://oei.es/salactsi/Livro_CTS_OEI.pdf

Brasil. (2019). Política Nacional da Erva-Mate. http://www.planalto.gov.br/ccivil_03/_ato2019-2022/2019/lei/L13791.htm

Chaimsohn, F.P., and Souza, A.M. de. (2012). *Sistemas de produção tradicionais e agroflorestais de erva-mate no centro-sul do Paraná e norte catarinense: Contribuições para a construção de um processo de indicação geográfica*. [The editors].

Dagnino, R. (2019). *Tecnociência solidária: Um manual estratégico*. Lutas Anticapital.
Dias, R. (2011). O que é a política científica e tecnológica? *Sociologias*, 13(28), 316–344. https://doi.org/10.1590/S1517-45222011000300011
Dias, R. (2021). Tecnologia e poder: Uma interpretação da tecnologia como elemento fundamentalmente político. *Revista Tecnologia e Sociedade*, 17(46), 55–72. https://doi.org/10.3895/rts.v17n46.12278
Dirección General de Estadística Encuestas y Censos. (2020). *Compendio Estadístico—2018*. DGEEC. https://www.ine.gov.py/Publicaciones/Biblioteca/documento/2edf_Compendio%20Estadistico%20Ambiental%202018.pdf
Embrapa Florestas. (2017). *Cultivo da Erva-Mate*. Second ed. Embrapa Florestas. https://www.spo.cnptia.embrapa.br/home
Embrapa Florestas. (2020). Erva-mate XXI: Inovação e Tecnologias para o Setor Ervateiro. https://www.embrapa.br/florestas/busca-de-eventos/erva-mate-evento-online
Escobar, A. (2011). Ecología Política de la globalidad y la diferencia. In: H. Alimonda (Org.), *La Naturaleza Colonizada. Ecología Política y Minería en América Latina* (pp. 61–92). CLACSO.
Escobar, A. (2014). *Sentipensar con la tierra: Nuevas lecturas sobre desarrollo, territorio y diferencia*. Ediciones Unaula.
Feenberg, A. (2010). Racionalização subversiva: Tecnologia, poder e democracia. In: R.T. Neder (Org.), *A teoria crítica de Andrew Feenberg: Racionalização democrática, poder e tecnologia* (pp. 67–95). Observatório do Movimento pela Tecnologia Social na América Latina/CDS/UnB/Capes.
Gerhardt, M. (2013). História ambiental da erva-mate [Doctoral dissertation, Universidade Federal de Santa Catarina]. https://repositorio.ufsc.br/handle/123456789/107480
Instituto Brasileiro de Geografia e Estatística. (2019). *Censo Agropecuário 2017*. IBGE. https://censos.ibge.gov.br/agro/2017/
Instituto Brasileiro de Geografia e Estatística. (2020a). *Produção Agrícola Municipal—PAM 2019*. IBGE. https://www.ibge.gov.br/estatisticas/economicas/agricultura-e-pecuaria/9117-producao-agricola-municipal-culturas-temporarias-e-permanentes.html?=&t=o-que-e
Instituto Brasileiro de Geografia e Estatística. (2020b). *Produção da Extração Vegetal e da Silvicultura—PEVS 2019*. IBGE. https://www.ibge.gov.br/estatisticas/economicas/agricultura-e-pecuaria/9105-producao-da-extracao-vegetal-e-da-silvicultura.html?=&t=o-que-e
Instituto Federal de Santa Catarina. (2020). Webnário Araucária e Erva-mate. https://www.youtube.com/channel/UC0rhN77XA0ZXQlXRoWWzBdg
Instituto Nacional de la Yerba Mate. (2021). *Informe del Sector Yerbatero—Diciembre de 2020*. INYM. https://www.inym.org.ar/publicaciones/informe-del-sector-yerbatero/
Luiz, R.G. (2017). Conservação da biodiversidade, cultivo e produção de erva-mate no município de São Mateus do Sul-PR [Master's thesis, Universidade Tecnológica Federal do Paraná]. http://repositorio.utfpr.edu.br/jspui/handle/1/2955
Marques, A. da C. (2014). As paisagens do mate e a conservação socioambiental: Um estudo junto aos agricultores familiares do Planalto Norte Catarinense [Doctoral dissertation, Universidade Federal do Paraná]. http://hdl.handle.net/1884/35824
Mazuchowski, J.Z., and Rucker, N.A. (1997). *Erva-Mate—Prospecção Tecnológica da Cadeia Produtiva. Documento Executivo* (1a, p. 27). Secretaria de Estado da Agricultura e do Abastecimento do Paraná.
Nimmo, E.R., Carvalho, A.I. de, Laverdi, R., and Lacerda, A.E.B. (2020). Oral history and traditional ecological knowledge in social innovation and smallholder sovereignty: A case study of erva-mate in Southern Brazil, *Ecology and Society*, 25(4), art17. https://doi.org/10.5751/ES-11942-250417

Nogueira, J.F.M.M. (2021). Historicidade e significado nas paisagens dos sistemas tradicionais de produção de erva-mate na bacia do Alto Iguaçu, sul do Paraná [Master's thesis, Universidade Estadual de Ponta Grossa]. http://tede2.uepg.br/jspui/handle/prefix/3379

Oliveira, Y.M.M. de, and Rotta, E. (1985). *Área de distribuição natural de erva-mate (Ilex paraguariensis St. Hil.).* pp. 17–36. http://ainfo.cnptia.embrapa.br/digital/bitstream/item/102798/1/AreaDistribuicao.pdf

Paraná, G. do E. do. (2018). *Política Estadual de Incentivo à Erva-Mate.* https://www.legislacao.pr.gov.br/legislacao/pesquisarAto.do?action=exibir&codAto=205493&indice=1&totalRegistros=1&dt=27.7.2021.22.16.37.895

Penteado Junior, J.F., and Goulart, I.C.G. dos R. (2019). *Erva 20: Sistema deprodução para erva-mate.* Embrapa. https://www.embrapa.br/busca-de-publicacoes/-/publicacao/1106677/erva-20-sistema-de-producao-para-erva-mate

Raffestin, C. (1993). *Por uma geografia do poder.* Editora Ática.

Saquet, M.A. (2017). *Consciência de classe e de lugar, práxis e desenvolvimento territorial.* Consequência Editora.

Saquet, M.A. (2020). *Abordagens e concepções de território.* Fifth ed. Consequência Editora.

7 Multiple territorialities in Pampa del Indio, Argentina (2011–2021)

Malena Castilla

Introduction

This chapter explains how the implementation of road and water development projects reveals conflicts and territorialities, power relations, confrontations, and resistance emerging in territory. We are interested in explaining territorial processes emerging from power relations, domination, incorporation, and resistance due to disputes over the use, control, and access to common goods and cultural knowledge. These disputes occur among local inhabitants, national and international entrepreneurs, foundations, governmental organisations, and international credit agencies. This is a case study showing the economic rationality behind the advancement of extractive projects. It is relevant to note that the infrastructure projects mentioned (water and roads) were not subject of prior consultations or environmental impact reports.

The chapter is divided into five sections. The second section contains a brief description of the case study, located in the locality of Pampa del Indio, in the Province of Chaco. This description includes relevant demographic, spatial, and productive characteristics of the area. The third section explains the methodology and research techniques used. This is a long-term research project that began with undergraduate studies and continued through a post-doctoral stage. The fourth section presents the key concepts that support the analysis, highlighting territory, development, power, and accumulation. The fifth section explains how infrastructure works have mainly served national and transnational entrepreneurs who monopolise value chains, as they increase agribusiness productivity, while generating processes of land accumulation. Finally, the chapter ends with the conclusions in the sixth section.

Case study

Since 2011, the Province of Chaco has been the setting for the implementation of various public policies and development projects related to territorial planning, financed by international credit agencies such as the World Bank. In this chapter, we focus on two main infrastructure projects: the road

DOI: 10.4324/9781032650241-9

improvement called Provincial Route No. 3, and the hydraulic infrastructure works that lead to the tourist project called 'The Qom Culture Route' (RCQ). The RCQ arises from the works of infrastructure development carried out by the Ministry of Public Works, and the joint work with local foundations, associations, and indigenous population.

Pampa del Indio, located in the northwest of the Province of Chaco, is part of the Libertador General José de San Martín department, and is separated from the province of Formosa by the Bermejo River (see Figure 7.1). Chaco is located in the northeast of the Argentine Republic and is part of the so-called Chaco Region.

The most recent data shows that Pampa del Indio had a population of 15,287 according to the 2010 census, with 9,204 residents in the urban area and 6,083 in the rural area (INDEC, 2012). The urban area serves as the town's commercial and administrative hub, housing markets, the municipality (local authorities), the hospital, and other essential services and commercial spaces. This central area is predominantly inhabited by individuals who identify as criollos and gringos, living in houses that meet basic living standards.

On the outskirts of the administrative centre lies the Old Town, the original settlement area, where both criollos and members of the Qom indigenous community (in the Toba neighbourhood) reside. Although living conditions here are more precarious, some houses have basic services and better access

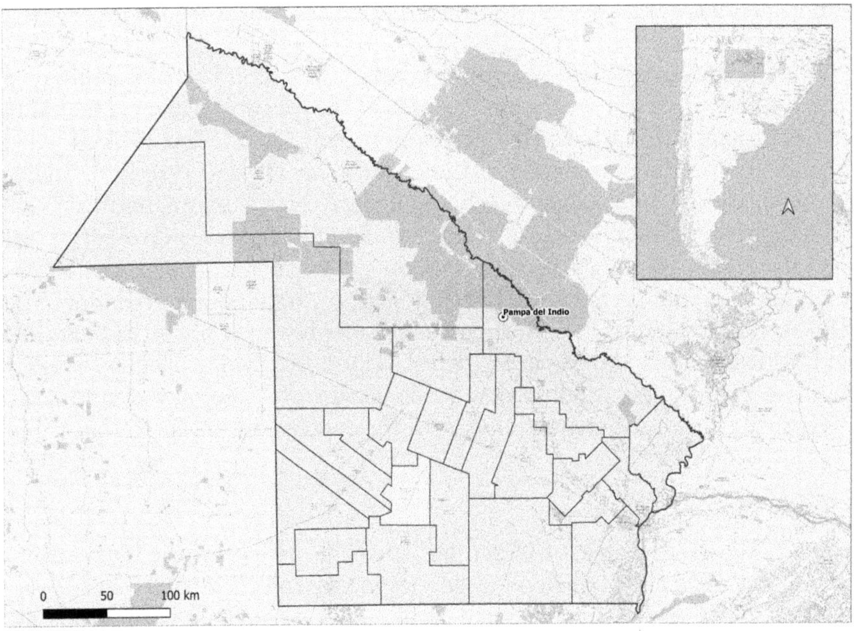

Figure 7.1 Map of the Province of Chaco in the Argentine Republic. Author.

to the town's administrative centre. Describing the socio-economic, cultural, and historical characteristics of the communities of Pampa del Indio requires a broad approach that we cannot undertake in this chapter (see Castilla, 2019), but we can provide a general overview. Most recent available data shows that the population inhabiting rural areas is largely composed of members of indigenous communities of the Qom people. Their homes are scattered along the territory delimited by Provincial Route No. 3. In this area, close to 50% of the population resides in extremely precarious conditions (INDEC, 2012). Many of their homes are built with mud, sheet metal, plastics, and other unsuitable materials, lacking sewerage or drinking water services. Some residents have cisterns that allow them to accumulate water on rainy days or store water when the municipal truck distributes it to homes. In Pampa del Indio, the percentage of unsatisfied basic needs (UBN) rises to 39%, while 47% of the population lives below the poverty line. 65% of the population lacks sewerage, and 33% lacks access to drinking water (INDEC, 2012). Chaco is the fifth province with the most urgent water scarcity, which is paradoxical, considering that the area is surrounded by two rivers: the Bermejo and the Guaycurú.

However, despite the water scarcity experienced by the local population, national and transnational entrepreneurs continue to establish agribusiness firms in the region, requiring large amounts of land and water. The 2018 Agricultural Census in the Province of Chaco showed that 92% of the hectares are destined for agricultural use. A large part of that land is used for oilseed production and livestock breeding, allowing Chaco to rank fourth and fifth in the provincial ranking in this type of production at the national scale. In 2020, the areas planted with soybeans in the province covered 542,973 hectares (Ministerio de Agricultura, Ganadería y Pesca, n.d.).

In Pampa del Indio, fences separate the private fields from indigenous communities and small producers. These boundaries, however, are not static. Each year they are moved and expanded, annexing more land for agribusiness through the purchase, sale, and leasing of fields. That public land, which the provincial state is responsible for commercialising, is often taken from the province's ancestral inhabitants (Castilla, 2020a). Thus, the territory is constantly changed by fences, the establishment of agribusiness, and the infrastructural development that such businesses require. Observed changes include the drying up of streams and ponds and the deterioration of native species such as the Quebracho tree, used to prepare traditional foods, which has stopped producing seeds. Similarly, Chaguar plants have stopped growing as a result of intense fumigation in the area (Castilla, 2021). As we will see in the following pages, these territorial transformations have not only transformed nature but also the dynamics of daily life.

In the face of poverty and territorial exploitation, international credit agencies such as the World Bank, financed development policies to promote regional development, increase local productivity, and commercialise agricultural products in international markets. Interventions in the region have not been scarce. Other programmes aimed to incorporate some community members into the value chain, integrating them into the markets, as argued in interviews (field notes, 2019). On the other hand, public investment, responsibility of the National and Provincial Government of Chaco, focused on road improvement works, water infrastructure, and cultural management in different parts of the province.

Methodology

This is a case study conducted throughout ten years in the locality of Pampa del Indio. The fieldwork included in-depth interviews, participant and non-participant observation, field notes, and recordings. In addition, the research used secondary sources such as documents prepared by credit agencies and government agencies, websites containing relevant information by the same actors that are deployed in the territory, and news published in local newspapers. Due to the mandatory social isolation imposed in Argentina as a strategy to mitigate the COVID-19 pandemic, some interviews took place through virtual platforms or telephone conversations. The fact of having built previous bonds with the local actors facilitated the remote work and, although in-person relationships cannot be equated with online tools, constant communication allowed us to maintain connection and know part of the reality that occurs in the territory. The interviews or records referred to in this document do not contain proper names and specific functions exercised by the actors, to maintain and prioritise the anonymity of the participants.

Territoriality, development and land grabbing

We understand territory from a multidimensional perspective, that is, as a space where land and social subjects are linked, a space where objects and actions converge and become inseparable and indivisible (Santos, 2006). In this sense, the objects shape the actions, and the actions allow the consolidation of new objects, constantly transforming the space. Human beings perform a large part of these actions; therefore, the relationships they establish with each other and with nature have a greater influence on territorial transformation and configuration. According to Mançano, 'the space is formed by elements of nature and social dimensions, produced by relations between people, such as culture, politics, and economy. People produce spaces' (2005, p. 26). This idea of territory is closely linked to the idea of power and its exercise, meaning that multiple scales, possibilities, properties, relationships, and conflicts converge in a territory (Mançano, 2009). Power relations also shape and transform territories, and in Pampa del Indio this has meant the expansion and destruction of actions and relationships. Agribusiness expansion over indigenous and peasant territories has also brought up new technologies, labour relations, and infrastructure development resulting, on many occasions, in the expulsion of population and the destruction of territories.

These are appropriation dynamics that de-territorialise ancestral populations; however, multiple territorialities can also occur, for example, through resistance (Mançano, 2005).

The expansion and accumulation of capital have given rise to processes of accumulation by dispossession (Harvey, 2004), land grabbing, and nature appropriation (Borras and Franco 2013) in the region. However, Chaco shows that accumulation does not occur only through dispossession. Incorporation, that is, the expansion over lands and commons, including the beings that inhabit them, to implement different projects such as agribusiness (mainly), and driven by provincial and national entities, international organisations, foundations, and civil society associations (Giraldo, 2015). 'The occupants of the lands are included in the projects through a variety of institutional arrangements that are generally averse to them' (Borras and Franco 2013, p. 95). Thus, the region experiences a process of deterritorialisation not only by the accumulation of land through dispossession but also its rearrangement and the installation of new logics of being and inhabiting the territory, in pursuit of economic gains (Haesbaert 2013; Harvey, 2004; Leff, 2005). As we will see in Chaco, the various strategies implemented not only have resulted in territorial appropriation by some agribusiness actors but also involve 'new forms of territorial control that ultimately fall under the authority of a handful of capitalists' (Giraldo, 2015, p. 651).

Certainly, much of this 'handful of capitalists' settled in the territories and expanded their activities through alliances and agreements established with other actors (Svampa, 2019). In parallel, development projects served to maximise profits while controlling potential conflicts that may arise with the local communities. According to Manzanal (2014), development projects are territorialised to generate proximity between the actors involved, articulate trade and the global market, and achieve a certain degree of social cohesion. However, in this case, the actors involved (whether the state at its different levels, credit agencies, foundations, and/or local actors) vie for the use, access, and control of territories, making 'it impossible to ignore the power and domination relations present in the territories (…) [demonstrating that] the social production of space is nothing more than the result of the exercise of power' (Manzanal, 2014, pp. 28–31). Thus, development policies and projects are implemented through power concealed under discourses of progress, investments, and sustainability (Leff, 2005; Santos, 2014), while constituting a necessary denial to achieve objectives and results (Manzanal 2014). What is denied in Chaco are the history and problems that a large part of the population experience, which are systematically minimised or made invisible to implement policies that allow new ways of ordering the territory through agribusinesses (Castilla, 2020a). The promises of 'development' and better life quality are often made by the same actors linked to dominant economic sectors. Far from solving conflicts, they deepen them by bringing false solutions to real problems (Escobar, 2012; Esteva, 2009; Saquet, 2015; Salamanca Villamizar and Pizarro, 2016).

The following sections will show how power relations, domination, and resistance are configured to dispute the control and use of commons and the territory. In short, we will see that the territory is a space of confrontation and exercise of powers.

Results and discussion: Increased productivity and incorporation of the local population

This section explains how infrastructure projects create processes of territorialisation and deterritorialisation facilitated by asymmetric power relations. These projects have international financing, are executed through national and provincial governments, and involve the local population through a plan called the 'Indigenous Peoples Plan'. However, this research shows that beyond addressing local needs, the projects seek to mitigate possible conflicts and increase production and economic gains. It is in this scenario that the population resists and negotiates.

Regional integration and International development projects

Over the past two decades, international organisations like the World Bank and the Inter-American Development Bank have funded projects to improve road connectivity and boost production in northern Argentina. These initiatives, supported by territorial planning policies and various water infrastructure works, involved actions across the region with the help of foundations, associations, and NGOs. Before delving into this, it's important to contextualise these policies within the broader framework of Argentina's regional integration efforts.

With the creation of the Union of South American Nations (UNASUR) in 2008,[1] actions aimed at territorial planning and increasing agricultural production became more prominent in Argentina. The agreements included establishing sectoral councils at the ministerial level, such as the South American Council of Infrastructure and Planning (COSIPLAN), which aimed to identify and select high-impact projects for South America's integration and development. A significant outcome was the Initiative for the Integration of South American Regional Infrastructure (IIRSA), which sought to modernise physical infrastructure from a regional perspective (Comunicado de Brasilia, 2000).

Within this framework and with financing from the World Bank, a series of interconnected projects were implemented in 2011 through IIRSA to enhance productivity, competitiveness, and commercialisation for agribusiness in Chaco province. These projects include the Road Infrastructure Project for the Development of the Northern Region (BIRF 7991AR) and the water infrastructure project (BIRF 7992AR) (Castilla, 2020b).

The BIRF 7991AR project received 400 million US dollars for improvements, expansion, and rehabilitation of the regional road network. Paved routes included Provincial Route No. 3, linking Pampa del Indio, Villa Rio Bermejito, and later El Espinillo, providing access to other national and

Figure 7.2 Image showing the road infrastructure works on the provincial Route No. 3. Photograph taken during fieldwork in December 2021.

international corridors (Figure 7.2). Much of this work was conducted in areas with agribusiness enterprises, particularly those with 'cash crops' destined for raw materials or finished products (Borras and Franco 2013). Our research found that many producers in these areas are national and transnational companies that settled decades ago by displacing indigenous people and peasants. These companies are interconnected and exploit the territories, commons, and inhabitants of Chaco.

To increase productive potential, a series of water infrastructure works were financed and executed in the same areas where road networks were paved. Near the town of Pampa del Indio, a water treatment plant that draws water from the Bermejo River was built along with a network of aqueducts running along part of Route No. 3. These works had an investment of 200 million US dollars, intended to meet the needs of 35,000 inhabitants. However, despite the benefits of road paving and communal taps, much of the local population did not experience a substantial improvement in their quality of life.

The fact that these regional interventions are defined by multinational agreements illustrates how territories are both multidimensional and multiscalar. They are multidimensional as they encompass a wide diversity of relationships between space and its inhabitants (Santos, 2006; Mançano, 2005). They are multiscalar as transformative actions can originate from actors who are not necessarily physically present in the territory.

Boosting production with road networks and water infrastructure

During our visits to the countryside and interviews with local inhabitants, we observed that the paving of Route No. 3 improved transportation access. However, remote areas where the rural population resides remain unpaved. This paving, along with other projects like tunnelling, sewers, and dams, aimed at boosting local productivity, has had various consequences. A member of a foundation working in the area commented:

> The mega-projects that have been carried out in the last 15 years are all disastrous for the communities, for the management of water basins, and for managing events such as drought and flooding. And here I am not only referring to water, I also mean everything related to roads; a good part of the floods that occur today in the province of Chaco are due to the disaster they have made with road planning.
>
> (Interview with a foundation member, August 2020)

The waterworks included constructing aqueducts with communal taps located in schools, but these did not meet local demand during water scarcity emergencies, affecting much of the population. An official from the National Ministry overseeing the project argued that the technicians were inexperienced and made mistakes, such as placing taps inside schools, making them inaccessible when schools were closed (Telephone interview with a World Bank official, March 2020). Another World Bank interviewee confirmed this and added that the taps were often stolen (Figure 7.3). When we asked this technician about the Bank's response to these incidents, he replied:

> The bank's role was to supervise the project implementation … they told us about [the thefts] and how the communities said to leave only one tap to prevent stealing, as people won't take the only one, but if there are two people will steal one because the other one keeps on working.
>
> (interview with a World Bank technician, March 2020)

In other words, the international credit agency and the national and provincial organisations responsible for implementing public policies have chosen not to act, even when confronted with needs and neglect. However, despite these political decisions, we wanted to determine if the remaining taps were sufficient to meet the population's needs:

> I don't know what pipes they made, there are some taps that are public, in the school in Campo Medina.… These are public taps … so that's a problem … because sometimes there are many of us, sometimes the taps are broken.
>
> (member of the Qom community of Castilla, 2019)

Figure 7.3 Image showing a damaged water tap installed inside a school. Photograph taken during fieldwork in December 2021. Author.

The above leads us to determine that the main concern of these projects is to increase production and commercialisation. Indeed, ensuring water access and control, and developing a road network to reduce transportation times and costs, is crucial for entrepreneurs as it allows more efficiency and expansion. In early 2021, the repaving of the section connecting Route No. 3 with Route No. 90 was announced; coincidentally, this improvement supports a private agribusiness farm (Chaco Day by Day, 2021). This same farm also receives irrigation water from the Bermejo River through various government-funded infrastructure works and falls within the area influenced by World Bank-funded projects.

It is important to note that entrepreneurs in this area expand their territories by purchasing and leasing land, as well as through the exercise of power and clientelist practices. For example, by conducting illegal fumigations that encroach on indigenous territories and small producers. Crop-dusting planes spray agrochemicals, causing illness among local inhabitants, destroying biodiversity, and contaminating soil, groundwater, and water basins. This has forced some of the population to abandon their territories after years of disputes. Clientelist practices include distributing water in tanker trucks. Due to the lack of secure water sources, the rural population often relies on rainwater collected in cisterns and tanks in an area with scarce rainfall. Consequently, municipalities and private actors transport and distribute water in tanker trucks. These are examples of how the territory becomes a space for exercising power. Disputes between actors with diverse interests and unequal power relations generate multiple territorialities through expulsion and appropriation (Harvey, 2004; Borras and Franco 2013; Giraldo, 2015). When economically or politically powerful actors intervene in territories inhabited by historically marginalised populations, processes of expulsion and appropriation are common (Mançano, 2005).

Indigenous Peoples Plan: Incorporation, mitigation, and conflict containment

The infrastructure projects included a special consultation programme in accordance with World Bank regulations, which mandate working with the population affected by the projects. In this case study, both the road networks and the waterworks pass through territories inhabited by indigenous communities and small producers. Following a community consultation organised by members of the Bank, government agencies, and local foundations, the Indigenous Peoples Plan was developed. This plan included a project to address problems identified by the community, such as accident prevention, road safety garbage disposal, and noise. Additionally, a series of economic projects were launched to benefit the communities and mitigate potential negative impacts of the works, such as promoting productive activities and providing equipment and machinery for production and marketing of traditional products.

However, conflicts related to the infrastructure works persisted despite these measures. For example, news of accidents on the newly paved road led to several community demonstrations demanding measures to prevent further incidents. Although this area has relatively few accidents compared to others in the country, media coverage of these incidents has become frequent, as have the protests by the affected communities. Agricultural producers benefiting from the territorial works also demonstrated demanding the maintenance of the road and security for their transportation activities.

The participation of indigenous peoples in the formulation and execution of territorial development projects is a strategy adopted by government agencies and organisations such as the World Bank to ensure the success of the projects, that is, to guarantee that the projects are carried out without creating conflicts. This strategy consists in creating participatory and consultation spaces with community members to provide information about the project, identify needs, and seek the community's approval to move forward. The communities are not consulted about the feasibility of the projects, but only about what benefits they would like to have in exchange for the implementation of the works in their territories. Therefore, these consultations are not mechanisms for the community to express their concerns and positions about the project but rather to express their needs in general. In this way, the communities are made part of the process but have no voice in determining whether the project will be executed and how.

The Indigenous Peoples Plan also included projects such as promoting productive activities and commercialising traditional products. However, these projects did not ensure the sustainability of these activities, leading to exploitation of natural resources. For example, the plan included cultivating yerba mate, reforesting with native species, and planting fruit trees. While these activities are traditional, they have been integrated into the market economy and require land and resource use.

Conclusions

The case highlights the multidimensional and power-driven nature of territory, emphasiing that territory is a space where land and social subjects are interconnected, shaped by natural and social elements, and influenced by the actions and relationships of its inhabitants. Power dynamics significantly impact territorial transformation, as evidenced in Pampa del Indio, where agribusiness expansion has led to both the development and destruction of territories. This expansion introduces new technologies and infrastructure, often resulting in the displacement of populations and destruction of spaces. Processes of land grabbing and nature appropriation are facilitated by international and national entities, leading to both dispossession and incorporation of lands for economic gains. On the other hand, local communities engage in resistance and negotiation to cope with the changes brought by development projects. Despite measures to incorporate indigenous peoples into development projects, conflicts persist, demonstrating the ongoing struggle for control and use of territories.

Development projects frequently involve local populations through strategies aimed at mitigating conflicts, but these do not necessarily ensure effective participation or sustainability. The Indigenous Peoples Plan, while aiming to address community needs and promote productive activities, failed to guarantee long-term sustainability and equitable decision-making. Infrastructure projects, such as road networks and water infrastructure, are primarily focused on increasing productivity and economic gains rather than addressing local needs. These projects often result in territorial appropriation and new forms of control by a few capitalists, exacerbating conflicts and social tensions.

The exercise of power in territories is evident in the various forms of appropriation, resistance, and conflict. Territorial development projects are often implemented through power dynamics concealed under discourses of progress and sustainability, neglecting the historical and social complexities of the affected populations, who also exercise a form of power through their resistance.

Note

1 Argentina, Bolivia, Brasil, Chile, Colombia, Ecuador, Guyana, Paraguay, Perú, Surinam, Uruguay, and Venezuela.

Bibliography

Borras, S.M., and Franco, J.C. (2013). Global land grabbing and trajectories of agrarian change: A preliminary analysis, *Journal of Agrarian Change*, 12(1), 34–59.

Castilla, M. (2020b). Políticas de desarrollo (in)sostenible en Pampa del Indio, Chaco (Argentina), *Pampa: Revista Interuniversitaria de Estudios Territoriales*, (22), 21–39.

Castilla, M. (2021). "Acá nunca llueve y en el campo del al lado llueve todos los días": Una descripción sobre el uso y acceso a las tierras y el agua en Chaco, *Folia História del Nordeste*, (41).

Castilla, M.I. (2019). *Procesos de reactualización identitaria, territorial y políticas de desarrollo entre las organizaciones indígenas del pueblo qom en la localidad de Pampa del Indio, provincia del Chaco.* Buenos Aires: Tesis doctoral Facultad de Filosofía y Letras (UBA).

Castilla, M.I. (2020a). Políticas de desarrollo y ordenamiento territorial: un análisis acerca de la vinculación de agencias internacionales, organismos gubernamentales y no gubernamentales y población indígena, *Mana*, 26(1) e261203.

Chaco día por día. (2021). *Concluyó la repavimentación de la Ruta N° 3, desde la Ruta 90 al campo de Eurnekián*, 4 de mayo de 2021. https://www.chacodiapordia.com/2021/05/04/concluyo-la-repavimentacion-de-la-ruta-no-3-desde-la-ruta-90-al-campo-de-eurnekian/

Comunicado de Brasilia. 2000. Available at http://www.iirsa.org/admin_iirsa_web/Uploads/Documents/comunicado_brasilia_esp.pdf

Escobar, A. (2012). Más allá del desarrollo: postdesarrollo y transiciones hacia el pluriverso, *Revista de antropología social*, 21, 23–62.

Esteva, G. (2009). La crisis como esperanza, *Bajo el volcán*, 14(8).

Giraldo, O.F. (2015). Agroextractivismo y acaparamiento de tierras en América Latina: una lectura desde la ecología política, *Revista mexicana de sociología*, 77(4), 637–662.

Haesbaert, R. (2013). Del mito de la desterritorialización a la multiterritorialidad, *Cultura y representaciones sociales*, 8(15), 9–42.

Harvey, D. (2004). *El nuevo imperialismo* (Vol. 26). Ediciones Akal.

Instituto Nacional de Estadísticas y Censos (INDEC). (2012). *Censo Nacional de Población, Hogares y Viviendas 2010* (p. 281). Argentina: Tomo 1.

Leff, E. (2005). La geopolítica de la biodiversidad y el desarrollo sustentable, *Revista del Observatorio Social de América Latina*, 17, 185–209.

Mançano, B. (2005). Movimientos socio-territoriales y socio-espaciales: contribución teórica a una lectura geográfica de los movimientos sociales, *Revista Nera*, (6), 24–34.

Mançano, B. (2009). *Sobre a tipologia de territórios. Territórios e territorialidades: teorias, processos e conflitos*. São Paulo: Expressão Popular, pp. 197–215.

Manzanal, M. (2014). Desarrollo, una perspectiva crítica desde el análisis del poder y del territorio, *Realidad económica*, 283.

Ministerio de Agricultura, Ganadería y Pesca. (n.d.). Estimaciones Agrícolas. Retrieved from https://datosestimaciones.magyp.gob.ar/

Salamanca Villamizar, C., and Astudillo Pizarro, F. (2016). Justicia(s) espacial(es) y tensiones socio-ambientales. Desafíos y posibilidades para la etnografía de un problema transdisciplinario, *Etnografías Contemporáneas*, 2(3), 24–54.

Santos, C. (2014). Naturalismos y acumulación por desposesión. paradojas del desarrollo Sustentable, *Horizontes Antropológicos*, (41), 331–356.

Santos, M. (2006). *A natureza do espaço: técnica e tempo, razão e emoção. 2. reimpr.* Editora da Universidade de São Paulo, p. 1.

Saquet, M.A. (2015). *Por una geografía de las territorialidades y las temporalidades: una concepción multidimensional orientada a la cooperación y el desarrollo territorial.* Universidad Nacional de La Plata, Facultad de Humanidades y Ciencias de la Educación (UNLP - FaHCE).

Svampa, M. (2019). *Neoextractivismo y Desarrollo. En: Las fronteras del neoextractivismo en América Latina: conflictos socioambientales, giro ecoterritorial y nuevas dependencias* (p. 144). transcript Verlag.

8 Building biocultural territories in the *Solares* of the Yucatán Peninsula, Mexico

Ana Julia Cabrera Pacheco

Introduction

The Yucatán Peninsula has been inhabited for over ten thousand years by Maya peoples (Nigh & Ford, 2019). A key strategy behind this continuity is their multiple use of the territory: the *milpa*, a traditional agricultural system based on polyculture under swidden agriculture; the *solar* as a livelihood system; and the *monte* as an extended system to complement production (López Barreto et al., 2018; Pérez Ruiz, 2018; Toledo & Barrera-Bassols, 2008b). In Latin American indigenous tradition, the territory is an inherent part of culture, necessary for biological and social continuity (Estrada Lugo et al., 1998), and it is within territorial self-sufficiency that Maya peoples' autonomies are historically sustained (Duarte Duarte, 2018).

The *solar* is a basic territorial unit for the lives of Yucatecan Maya families. These populations connect with the territory through actions of preservation, enrichment, and dissemination of knowledge and practice. The *solar* is part of a complex system of land, livelihoods, and identities, maintained over time by Yucatecan Maya people through historical and contemporary processes of transformation, adaptation, and resistance. The *solar* is what it is today, thanks to the continuous relationship of Maya populations with the territory they inhabit and their strategies of multiple use of the territory. The territory has evolved through interventions by Maya populations over time, becoming a space in constant evolution and change (Cabrera Pacheco, 2017; Nigh & Ford, 2019).

The *solar* is also where Maya autonomy and sovereignty are manifested, largely based on everyday practices and self-subsistence within their domestic spaces and territories. In these spaces, biocultural territories are formed (Cabrera Pacheco, 2017; Colectivo Suumil Mookt'an, 2022; Duarte Duarte, 2014, p. 260). Biocultural territories are geographical and symbolic spaces where indigenous peoples exercise their rights, supporting the continuation of their traditional ways of life through historical and contemporary experiences with nature, language, and culture (Argumedo, n.d.; Macías López 2021).

This chapter addresses the question: How are biocultural territories reproduced through the daily life of Maya families in the Yucatán Peninsula? I contribute to the conceptualisation of biocultural territories from a vision of

DOI: 10.4324/9781032650241-10

ma'alob kuxtal (good living or Buen Vivir in Yucatec Maya, based on translations by López Valentín et al. (2020) and Rosado-May & Poot (2020)), where the relationships between nature, culture, and ways of life serve as a basis for reflecting on the conceptualisation and formation of the territory in the regional context of the Yucatán Peninsula, considered a priority biocultural region (Toledo et al., 2014). In the first part of the chapter, I review the concepts of territory and bioculturalism, proposing Buen Vivir as an alternative to modernity/coloniality. Next, I present the methodology and the research location. Finally, I examine and analyse how bioculturalism is constructed from the *solar* and the daily life of Yucatecan Maya families, within their own worldview.

Conceptualising the territory

The decolonial approach of this chapter begins with recognising and questioning the construction of Latin America through violent processes of dispossession, exploitation, and commodification of its indigenous peoples and lands. A decolonial vision incorporates and reinforces the epistemologies and ontologies of these peoples, accumulated through inhabiting their lands and territories for hundreds and thousands of years (Dussel, 1994; Toledo & Barrera-Bassols, 2008a; Carrasco, 2020).

The territory contains biological, geographical, social, and political meanings inscribed in the memory, representations, and values, becoming a place of mediation between human beings and their culture (Medeiros, 2008). Its material and immaterial character requires an approach that recognises the plurality of its economic, cultural, and natural dimensions, and the multiplicity of practices, ideas, and social subjects that overlap and interweave within historical and geographical contexts (Halvorsen, 2019; Saquet, 2008). The territory is initially considered a cultural space of identification and belonging, which guarantees the continuity of the groups that inhabit it. It involves territorial processes of appropriation, domination, and production, which include power relations, identities, contradictions, inequalities, differences, transformations, continuities, and diverse networks (Estrada Lugo et al., 1998; Medeiros, 2008; Saquet, 2008).

López Sandoval et al. (2017) argue that in Latin America, the concept of territory helps to reveal power relations in space and time, triggered by disputes or negotiations between global and local forces, and expressed through actions and strategies of territorially anchored groups, based on different rationalities and worldviews. Territories are, therefore, spaces for the reproduction of life (Barbosa, 2021), containing diverse strategies of care for the sustainability of life, following the communities' own organisational structure, customs, traditions, language, worldviews, principles, and values (Huanacuni Mamani, 2010). Beyond academic discussions, the territory has provided groups whose existence is tied to their lived spaces the opportunity to express feelings, understandings, and struggles in collective demands, and to discover endogenous possibilities of change (Haesbaert, 2020; López Sandoval et al., 2017). These communities have a sense of territory as an ethnic collective space and often involve ontological resistance, opposition, defence, and affirmation (Escobar, 2015).

Currently, many indigenous peoples have ways of life closely related to the territory they inhabit, using and transforming ecosystems for centuries or even millennia (Boege, 2008). This generates material, practical, and cultural ties, in what Sinco Ramos (2015, pp. 13) defines as bioculturalism: 'the development of a people's culture in relation to the processes and characteristics of nature, where people and nature correlate'.

Therefore, in this chapter, I approach territory as the space where human life is reproduced in coexistence with nature, marked by relations of appropriation, domination, transformation, and adaptation under specific historical and geographical contexts. This conceptualisation is strengthened and enhanced by the inclusion of bioculturalism and a vision of Buen Vivir, which I explore in the following sections.

Indigenous people's territory and bioculturalism

Biocultural territories arise from the constant interaction between groups of people, communities, or societies and their natural environment over a long-term territorial occupation. Over time, a mutual adaptation develops between these societies and their local environment in a process of coevolution, with close relationships between the landscape, biodiversity, and specific productive systems (Boege, 2008; Maffi, 2018; Toledo et al., 2019). These systems, in turn, have substantially contributed to shaping these cultures (Bezaury Creel et al., 2015). This coevolution can be analysed from a co-territoriality, where the various facets of mega-diversity (ecosystemic, biological, cultural, linguistic, agroecological, and agrobiological) are manifested in contemporary biocultural territories loaded with memory (Vásquez-Dávila and Lope-Alzina, 2012).

Biocultural territories comprise knowledge, productive and recreational practices, collective consciousness, and, in general, diverse socio-cultural manifestations aimed at sustaining life within domesticated and adapted agrosystems. They include tangible and intangible elements like language, ceremonies, the use of herbs and medicinal plants, the conservation of native seeds, soil care and water management, gastronomy, among many others, designed to follow the temporal rhythm of nature and the continuous repetition of rituals (Barbosa, 2021; Calderón and Santiz, 2021; Sinco Ramos, 2015). Among the elements of biocultural territory are also the strategies of its multiple use. In the case of the Yucatán Peninsula, these multiple uses are the *milpa* and the *solar*, complex geographical systems of production and reproduction of life, forest systems or *montes*, Maya ceremonies as biocultural links of their cosmovision, and the creation of income from outside the communities (Ek Cohuo, 2020; López Barreto et al., 2018; Pérez Ruiz, 2018; Toledo and Barrera-Bassols, 2008b).

The complex bioculturalism is considered a political construct of resistance. For example, Mexico's 22 biocultural regions are central nuclei of indigenous territories, covering a total of 28 million hectares (14% of the national territory) and more than 6 million indigenous inhabitants (Boege, 2008; Toledo et al., 2014). New indigenous and peasant resistances defend ways of life based on bioculturalism, rooted in the territory (Boege, 2014; Morales Barragán, 2019). In the *milpas* and *solares*, nature is transformed by humans and, in turn, transforms individuals and communities. Indigenous and peasant populations are constructing meanings and building an identity through the management and conservation of the territory that surrounds them (González et al., 2021; Vásquez-Dávila and Lope-Alzina, 2012).

An alternative development from the territory

In Latin America, the rhetoric of modernity based on progress, development, and growth has been present since colonial times. It continues to be reproduced alongside colonialism, creating poverty, misery, and inequalities for certain populations (Mignolo, 2002). Through this coloniality/modernity pair, territories have been constructed in the Latin American region. This has resulted in the massive dispossession of ancestral territories and the exploitation of their inhabitants, confined in practices of control/domination, segregation, and exclusion by colonial and nationalist states (Pérez Salas, 2020; Ribeiro and Ponte, 2020). The rhetoric has also translated, for governments, into a vision of nature as a 'resource' available for exploitation (Svampa, 2012), creating a 'permanent tension [for indigenous peoples] between maintaining autonomous spaces to decide their ways of living and the pressures coming from various actors [...] to abandon forms of life and production considered anachronistic and distant from modernity' (Pérez Ruiz, 2018, p. 228). Public policies that seek to develop the culture, natural resources, and well-being of indigenous peoples without considering their territory as a necessary reference (Boege, 2008) are incomplete and challenge the indivisibility between populations and the territory they inhabit, as they disintegrate the communal and cultural life of indigenous communities, by excluding the bases of their subsistence, capacities, and knowledge (Huanacuni Mamani, 2010).

Against modernity/coloniality, decolonial thought promotes an ecology of knowledge that recognises diverse epistemologies and ontologies, such as Buen Vivir, an alternative to conventional development—or rather, as a series of alternatives to development (Carrasco, 2020; Gudynas and Acosta, 2011; Svampa, 2012). Buen Vivir 'raises the possibility of a path for human subsistence based on ancestral knowledge and respect for nature' (López Córdova and Marañón Pimentel, 2013, p. 57) and questions the approximations to development based on economic growth, as it creates environmental damage, individualism and the commodification of life (Gudynas, 2011; Huanacuni Mamani, 2010).

Buen Vivir entails the recovery of spaces and ways of life that were invaded or usurped, to be re-signified highlighting that territory and nature coexist in a relationship of respect, balance, and harmony among all that exists. Buen Vivir focuses on quality of life and has a communal vision based on the reproduction of daily life through territory and common goods (Barbosa, 2021; Calderón and Santiz, 2021; Gudynas, 2011; Huanacuni Mamani, 2010). Buen Vivir also implies the recognition of cultural, environmental, social, and economic dimensions, based on the right to the self-determination of indigenous peoples, developing their ways of life and oriented towards collective well-being (López Valentín et al., 2020).

In the Yucatán Peninsula, during the 'developmentalism' of the 19th and 20th centuries, dispossession of Maya populations was widespread in the name of 'modernity', alienating 'the natural resources of the Maya people, their cultivation practices, their rites, their ceremonies, and ways of inhabiting space' (Duarte Duarte, 2018, p. 39). Their language, knowledge, and practices were devalued and used less frequently in daily life (Duarte Duarte, 2018; Velázquez Solís, 2012). This brought about extensive negative impacts imposed by public policies distant from the realities and needs of Maya peoples, a situation that remains today. In recent years, the Peninsula's 'development' has prioritised real estate, tourist projects, and agribusiness (Flores and Deniau, 2019) that consume and exploit the labour force and territory of the Maya people (Cabrera Pacheco, 2017).

The Maya vision of *ma'alob kuxtal* refers to the harmony between nature and humanity, and calls for the improvement of life in human, moral, and spiritual values, emphasising the importance of the collective over the individual; *ma'alob kuxtal* is evidence of a living culture that manifests itself in the persistence of language and territory degradation (López Valentín et al., 2020, p. 466), and 'continues to support contemporary Maya ways of life' (Duarte Duarte, 2018, p. 36). Therefore, analysing and discussing the biocultural territories of the Yucatán Peninsula contributes to the vindication of ancestral knowledge and ways of life resulting from the millennia-long relationship between Maya communities and the land they inhabit. These processes of defence continue today against dispossession and capitalist accumulation, challenging colonialist, racist, and developmental impositions (Flores and Deniau, 2019; Torres-Mazuera, 2018; Colectivo Suumil Mookt'an, 2022).

Methods and research location

This is a qualitative research based on documentary exploration and field data collection, following the principles of a critical ethnographic approach. This implies building a continuous relationship of respect between the researcher and the participants, to achieve a co-construction of knowledge, as well as an understanding of the reconstruction by the participants of their own histories (Heyl, 2001; Jordan and Yeomans, 1995). My positionality 'was simultaneously an insider, outsider, both and neither' (Sultana, 2007, p. 377). I am a local person with Yucatecan Maya origins, although I grew up far from Maya communities and lived and worked in the city. I have an educational privilege but was able to establish with the participants that we were 'not quite the same, not quite the other' and exchange anecdotes and relevant information (Trinh, 1997, p. 418).

Field techniques included surveys, semi-structured interviews, and participant observation on tours of *solares*, plots, and *milpas*. First, I conducted a literature review on the concepts of territory and bioculturalism, focused on the Latin American region, as well as the concept of Buen Vivir, *ma'alob kuxtal*, and the Maya *Solar* to update and deepen my previous research. Second, fieldwork was conducted in the months of March and April 2021 in 11 communities in seven municipalities in the states of Yucatán and Quintana Roo (Figure 8.1).

The participants were women and men who work the land, and we covered topics such as *solar* characteristics, perception of territory and collectivity, women's work, and Maya culture. In total, based on convenience non-probability sampling (Otzen and Manterola, 2017), I had contact with 44 individuals, 41 interviews, 36 walkabouts of *solares*, 2 walkabouts of commercial gardens, and 5 walkabouts of agricultural plots. The combination of methods allowed both for obtaining comparable data and the expression of viewpoints in a freer manner and for exploring topics relevant to the participants. Participant observation during the walkabouts aimed to gather information on crops and practices, but also to complement the information shared by other methods for better interpretation and understanding. The names of the participants have been pseudonymised.

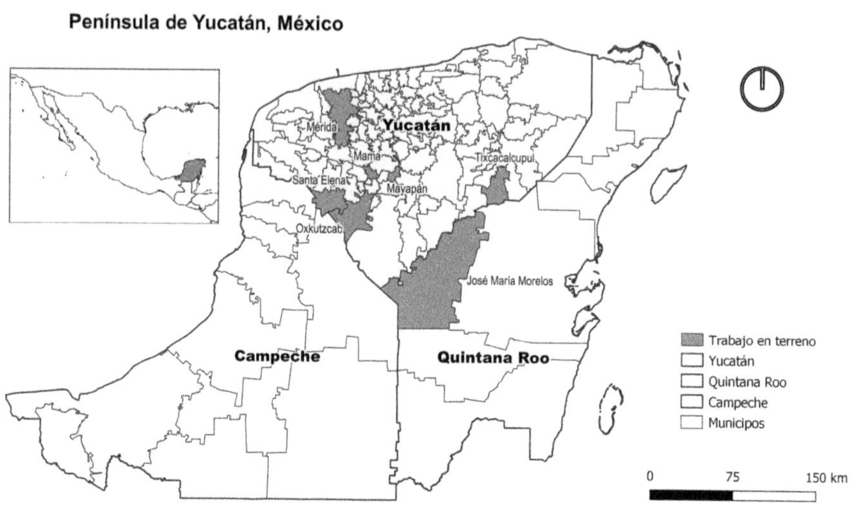

Figure 8.1 Yucatán Peninsula. Author.

Field visits were disrupted by the health emergency stemming from Covid-19. The original approach envisaged a gradual process of interaction with the participating individuals in the chosen communities. While the principles of critical ethnography remained, the implementation was adjusted to a single contact with the participants: the survey was adapted and included as the first part of the semi-structured interview, followed by a walkabout of the *solar* or agricultural plot. In some cases, only one or two of the activities were carried out. All participants are members of various working groups and organisations in the area, both in Yucatán and Quintana Roo, through which I contacted individuals from the communities to plan fieldwork. Trust through these contacts compensated for the affected plans of a gradual approach. It is worth noting that the current population (over 5 years old) that speaks an indigenous language is approximately 10% of the population of Campeche, 11% of Quintana Roo, and 23% of Yucatán (INEGI, 2020); therefore, some elements of the surveys and interviews conducted in Spanish contain words in Yucatec Maya (such as names of plants and foods). Particularly, in three communities, some interviews were conducted with simultaneous translation between Spanish and Yucatec Maya by women from the same communities; her names are Daniela Victoria Monte Peraza, Mariana Gutiérrez Poot, and María Consolación Puc Canul.

Methodologically, one of the main challenges in analysing the relationship of Maya populations in their *solares* with the territories they inhabit is that these experiences are neither representative nor exclusive regarding 'the hundreds of Maya communities of the Yucatán Peninsula [who] differ from each other in their history, subsistence patterns, levels of 'acculturation', organizational complexity, identity representation, nature of their relations with the dominant society, among others' (Quintal et al., 2003, p. 369).

The Maya biocultural territory of the Yucatán Peninsula

The Peninsula is located in southeastern Mexico, between the Gulf of Mexico and the Caribbean Sea, on the southern border with Belize and Guatemala, and comprises the states of Campeche to the west, Quintana Roo to the east, and Yucatán to the north. It is characterised by a flat and karstic topography, which leads to a lack of surface water and the presence of Cenotes. The region is mostly covered by deciduous jungle, developed on limestone and thin, rocky soil (Schmitter-Soto et al., 2002). In general, the environmental vulnerability of the region to the threats of climate change is defined by a high maritime influence, extreme hydrometeorological phenomena, and desertification processes (Orellana Lanza, 2015).

The historical construction of the *solar* (Cabrera Pacheco, 2017) dates to the 10th century, when emerged as scattered production spaces with a predominantly polyculture agricultural system under slash-and-burn cultivation. The violent Spanish domination altered the native spatial organisation, imposing a colonial rationalisation of space, which paradoxically physically configured the *solar* that we know today. Faced with colonial power, Maya families developed productive survival strategies, in some cases even regaining control of their ways of life by migrating to the eastern part of the Peninsula. However, commercial agricultural production in haciendas, between the end of the colonial period and during the 19th century, meant the accumulation of land and the new dispossession of Maya populations, who were violently integrated into the system as labour force, despite some strong resistances, in exchange for 'sufficient' land for the *milpa* and a space to live, the *solar*, where they had to intensify food production to survive. It wasn't until the 20th century, through land distribution processes, that the *solar* and its private and urban counterpart were recognised as livelihood strategies (ibid).

This history of dispossession of Maya communities continues today under neoliberal policies of individualisation, homogenisation, and commodification,[1] which are resisted and contained through strategies of defence and resilience of Maya peoples (Cabrera Pacheco, 2017). That is, in the *solar* as a dynamic system, both in its agrobiodiverse composition and in its cultural, socioeconomic, and historical processes, Maya families have demonstrated their resistance, adaptability, and resilience within their traditions (see García de Miguel, 2000; Hernández Sánchez, 2010; Jiménez-Osornio et al., 2015). Currently, the *solar* remains an important site for meeting the needs of Maya households through the continuity of daily life (Cabrera Pacheco, 2017; Jiménez-Osornio et al., 2015; Lope-Alzina, 2014).

Solares are the basic territorial unit for the habitation of peninsular Maya families (Figure 8.2) that contribute to providing cohesion to the family unit and the community, through actions of preservation, enrichment, and dissemination of knowledge that have allowed the survival of their ways of life (Cabrera Pacheco, 2014). Domestic spaces like the *solar* have been analysed 'as an existential condition of the need for adaptation and appropriation of the territory' (Sañudo Vélez, 2013, p. 225). Domestic spaces, privileged places of reproduction, production, and social invention, are physical, symbolic, and social entities of habitation whose practices contribute to the connection with the outside, with the collective and to the circularity of the territory, to its continuity and change (Collignon, 2010; Sañudo Vélez, 2013).

Traditionally, a *solar* has an area between 500 and 2,500 square metres, and up to 5,000 square metres (Cabrera Pacheco, 2014). In the information collected from 36 *solares* in the field, 7 were smaller than 500 square metres; 4 sized between 500 and 1,000; 16 sized between 1,000 and 2,500; 5 were larger than 2,500; and 1 had 8,000 square metres. Likewise, a traditional *solar* is composed of several spaces (Figure 8.2): the house (*casa-habitación*), the kitchen (*cocina*), the granary (*estancia*), the seedbed (*huerto*), the pigsty, the chicken coop (*gallineros*), the washing area (*área de lavado*), and the latrine or bathroom (*baño*). Various activities take place in the *solar*, both for production and reproduction of life, such as food preparation and intergenerational interaction. The survey shows that productive activities in *solares*,

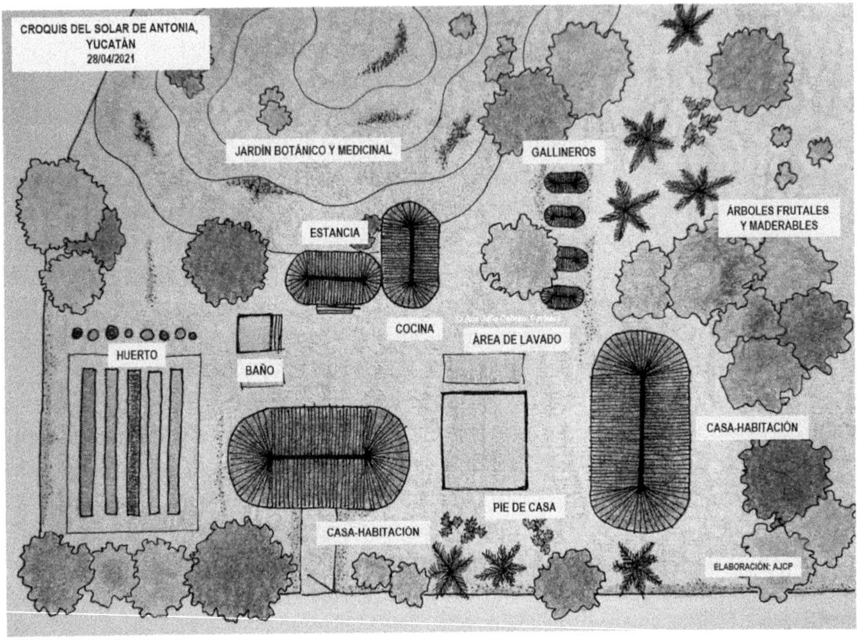

Figure 8.2 Maya *Solar*. Author.

milpas, and agricultural plots include 39 families growing vegetables, 36 raising domestic animals, 33 having fruit trees, 31 making seedbeds, 8 practising meliponiculture (farming of stingless bees), 19 engaging in some form of embroidery, and 23 weaving hammocks. Other activities include selling flowers, painting clothes, and selling food.

The role of women in *solar* production is of great importance, and therefore in the cultural reproduction of the region. The *milpa* and the *solar*, key elements of the biocultural territory, are differentiated spaces that generate distinct skills and knowledge between women and men (Pérez Ruiz, 2017). Women '... consider the solar as theirs and recognise its importance since it is the space where they mainly work, live ...' (Velázquez Solís, 2012, p. 70). *Solares* are also of great importance for the recovery and survival of the biocultural territory, as strategies are developed for the integral and sustainable use of resources, primarily generating self-sufficiency (Aké Gómez et al., 1999; Cabrera Pacheco, 2014; Correa Navarro, 1997). The *solar* 'includes a particular worldview and beliefs, knowledge, management practices, preferences for the management of particular species and groups of them that determine [its] composition' (Moreno-Calles et al., 2013, p. 377). *Solares* contain agrobiodiversity and preserve the socio-cultural systems that are created and utilise them daily (Bezaury Creel et al., 2015).

One of the contemporary physical representations of Maya culture manifests in the place they inhabit; it is in the *solar* as a geographical and symbolic space where Maya families continue with their traditional ways of life, interwoven with nature, their language, and culture, maintaining continuity in their daily lives. However, the *solar*, like the territory, is not a static space—it is a dynamic, organic, and changing space (Sañudo Vélez, 2013). Just as its historical construction was the result of transformations, it is also influenced by the different realities and manifestations of daily life for families and communities (Collignon, 2010). Some changes are generated by family growth within the finite space of the *solar*, the reduction of *solar* surface area due to public housing policies, and material losses caused by storms and hurricanes (see Cabrera Pacheco, 2017; and Wejebe Shanahan and Rodríguez Pavón, 2014).

Subsistence activities in the biocultural territory, as well as education and the generation of external income, are sustained by socially and spatially delimited family and social relations (Estrada Lugo et al., 1998). According to Calderón and Santiz (2021, p. 130), the *solar* 'enables the cultivation of food and other necessary activities to reproduce and sustain life, while the territory refers to the space of collective belonging', according to some reflections from the interviews:

> The most important thing for us Maya people is to take care of our territory because this territory is already ours ... if you know how companies are right now taking it away from us ... The territories are the forests, the water, the oxygen. Everything for me, the microorganisms, the people, are the main ones, it's our territory. It's our identity, as Mayas. All of that is linked to the territory, it's not like talking about an area, it's that in the area there is an abundance of wealth that we don't realize and many times we don't want to protect, for me, that's the territory.
>
> (Interview: Mateo, 77 years old, 04/27/2021)

> The territory is like where you can be and where you can develop, for me, that is territory. So practically the place where you are or where you would like to be is part of the territory. My territory, I think, would be my community because I know it well [...]. The territory of the community, I think it ... has a deeper meaning because it encompasses many things besides its extensions, the people who inhabit it, and it's what makes it your community.
>
> (Interview: Gloria, 23 years old, 03/03/2021)

During the interviews, some participants shared anecdotes and data about the activities they carry out in their *solar*es, reflecting some relationships between biodiversity and culture, and the knowledge about their territory, as well as some difficulties they experience:

> The radish doesn't take long, in a month and fifteen days it's ready, same with cilantro. Beets take three months, and tomatoes too … Everything is planted all year round, except corn, which is by season. [My mom] planted corn and saved the seeds, also lentils, also beans. […] And then we come and start watering before the sun comes out, we water everything. And then we start cooking for lunch, then, if we finish, we start weaving hammocks or sewing, if not, like right now we are seeing about the market, we fill the bags with soil and plant what we are going to sell.
>
> (Interview: Ana, 31 years old, 04/08/2021)

> I'm just starting my seedbed [of annatto], since I discovered that bees peck at it, it has a lot of pollen, produces a lot of pollen for the little bees. So I already made seedbeds, now that the rains start. Yes, they sprout [directly] but as now the drought is strong and the soil is very red here, they die on me. So I have it in the seedbed, and as soon as the rains come I'm going to transplant it.
>
> (Interview: Claudia, 35 years old, 04/26/2021)

> I left it because of the price of feed, I raised improved pigs and cattle, but they eat a lot. I don't have enough grass to feed them. Currently, I am starting with small ruminants like sheep, I am starting with four sheep and I see that it is more viable because in a garden we cannot be left without animals because they are a source of manure.
>
> (Interview: Mateo, 77 years old, 04/27/2021)

> Sometimes it doesn't work out, sometimes there are seasons when it doesn't work out and sometimes there are seasons when it does work out well. Sometimes we have to see how to do it. For example, this year there was almost nothing, the hurricane came …'
>
> (Interview: Antonia, 36 years old, 04/28/2021)

Within a 'biocultural and ethno-agroecological context' (Vásquez-Dávila and Lope-Alzina, 2012, p. 92), it is in the *Solar* where the relationship between knowledge and practice, knowledge and work, autonomy and sovereignty is expressed and manifested. The generation and transmission of knowledge, decision-making, and task execution are important components of *ma'alob kuxtal*:

> The advantage is that we can be freer if we work like this. We can be freer, so we can detach ourselves a bit from this neoliberal system and we can transform ourselves and take care of the environment.
>
> (Interview: Mateo, 77 years old, 04/27/2021)

> … I like to see, when you did your work, the work that it took, and it bears fruit, your vegetable, your fruit that you are working on. I like to

> see, no matter how small a plant is, and it is bearing fruit, this is, I planted it, I achieved it, it's my work. That satisfaction, that moves me, I like to see the result of what one does.
>
> (Interview: Elvira, 35 years old, 04/27/2021)

In these spaces, biocultural scenarios are constructed 'by transforming natural elements into biocultural resources, giving a specific identity to each of the social groups' (Vásquez-Dávila and Lope-Alzina, 2012, p. 297). From a decolonial perspective, it is the compatibility and complementarity of the domestic, of the Maya *solar*, with the biocultural territory that allows for the continuous reproduction of both (Nigh and Ford, 2019).

Ma'alob kuxtal as a key to the biocultural continuity of the territory

The *solar* is a key site for the transmission of knowledge, especially for women. As domestic spaces that are constructed day by day, traditional cultivation and animal husbandry techniques and knowledge of medicinal plants, sustainable water use, and local food preparation techniques are necessary. Beyond productive livelihoods in the *solares*, communities also reproduce many elements that maintain the worldview and territories of Maya peoples, both in their geographical and symbolic spaces, interweaving nature, language, and culture, maintain continuity in their daily lives. This continuity does not imply a return to the past but rather an articulation with modernity, appropriated, and adapted to the contexts, needs, and projects of Maya individuals, families, and communities (Velázquez Solís, 2012).

During the interviews, the participants all recognised themselves as Maya, giving some reasons to consider themselves part of the Maya people, or to be the Maya people, exemplifying some key elements, such as planting in the *solar* and the *milpa*, the use of the Maya language and its teaching to the new generations, the traditions and ceremonies of their ancestors, the knowledge related to medicinal plants, and the preparation of food with elements from the *solar* and the *milpa*. According to Velázquez Solís (2012), these practices and knowledge are ways of building and remaining in the *ma'alob kuxtal*, which reflect the essence of the Maya worldview. Below, I link some of these elements of *ma'alob kuxtal* with the reflections that emerged in the interviews.

> My mom has always [worked the land], when she married my dad, she was about 17 years old, she already worked it with my grandparents, because like my grandfather only had daughters, no sons, so they took her to the milpa with her sisters. In the milpa, she worked with my grandfather. They worked there, she has taught us many things, she has always liked it.
>
> (Interview: Ana, 31 years old, 04/08/2021)

> Well, I'm a farmer, I can tell you that it motivates me, I think it's for me a spiritual part, the spiritual part of the land has moved me a lot. It's something we brought from our ancestors, work is important, we don't see it, it's like an obligation, it's like food, [...], that can make us a little independent. By planting a little bit, [...] at least everything we do is a sign of resistance, it's like the revolution we are making. Showing that we can, with that, we can feel freer.
>
> (Interview: Mateo, 77 years old, 04/27/2021)

Nutrition and food sovereignty are also related to the territory one inhabits. For Maya families in the *solares*, food is prepared with elements harvested from their own territories (Dzib Hau, 2018):

> There [in the forest] we eat healthier things I say. Because there's everything, you have to eat chili, tomato, beans, there's everything in the forest. We were born there, also in the forest, my father was born there, not in the town. My favourite food is beans because you can make it different forms to eat, that's why I like it ... I put a little onion and a little lard, and uh! And a little chili'.
>
> (Interview: Arnulfo, 71 years old, 04/29/2021)

> ... we make what is called k'ol [for the] pibes that we make; [we make] a little hole in the dough and you put k'ol and hen or pork meat; there's no need to buy in the town [...]. You have your banana leaves, your hen, your pork, your lard, everything. You have all the things to make it yourself.
>
> (Interview: Marta, 45 years old, 19/04/2021)

Solares also help in preserving traditional ceremonies that reproduce the Maya worldview and cultural knowledge (Terán and Rasmussen, 2009):

> I always do it, last week I did an offering of saka'[2] for the land and for the little bees, mostly I do saka' offerings and we make waajicab[3] [or hanli cab] offerings, those are the ceremonies we do. It's something our grandparents left us and it's something we've found works. It's a belief, because we believe in what we do.
>
> (Interview: Mateo, 77 years old, 04/27/2021)

> Yes, tomorrow they are going to do a ceremony [waajil kool or u janli kol].[4] They make the k'ol,[5] a bucket of k'ol, they make little ball tortillas with pumpkin seed, put like three layers, cover it with boob leaf, and make a little hole and put it in there. And the k'olito is chicken with annatto, you put a little dough to make it hard. And the ya'ach',[6] don't you know how to say it in Spanish? You take out the tortillas and make them ya'ach' and put them in the chicken broth, that's separate and

that's what they present. And you prepare orange or watermelon juice. It's different from what is done in the milpa. You make the ch'a cháak,[7] it's almost the same, but it's different because it's done there [in the milpa]. The h'men[8] performs the ceremony'.

(Interview: María, 50 years old, 04/15/2021)

Paraphrasing Nora Tzec and Selena Uc from the Civil Association Ka' Kuxtal Much' Meyaj,[9] it is in and from the *solares* and the *milpa* where the Maya worldview is manifested and reproduced in family and community, and strengthened in their culture and identity, *ma'alob kuxtal* emerges and is maintained from the learning shared by grandparents, from the mother tongue, and that continues to today's practices, strengthened by the organisations that work with Maya communities in their well-being.

Conclusions

Throughout this chapter, I presented elements to construct the narrative of the daily construction of the territory from the bioculturality of the Maya families' *solares* in the Yucatan Peninsula. The *solar* is the basic territorial unit for the inhabiting of Maya peoples; it is a site of resistance that has been historically constructed for the subsistence of families. But this construction has not been isolated; it has been part of the integrated management of the territory carried out by these Maya communities, being strongly intertwined through historical and contemporary experiences with nature and culture, developing the biocultural geographical and symbolic spaces that I have presented in this chapter.

Threats to the territory are also threats to Maya domestic livelihoods, and the discontinuation of knowledge, the Maya language, and the daily life in the *solar* will impact the preservation of the territory by losing the multiplicity of uses and associated knowledge that have allowed its permanence and relevance. It is in the reproduction of practices, knowledge, and elements such as traditional cultivation techniques, knowledge, and use of medicinal plants, repetition of rituals, and continuity of traditional food preparation that this bioculturality is evident in the *solares*, and it is from these domestic daily practices that biocultural territories are shaped and constructed. The well-being and quality of life of *solar* inhabitants are linked to their environment, so the relationality, complementarity, and correspondence between *solar* and territory guarantee the *ma'alob kuxtal* of Maya communities and their biocultural territories.

Looking at the domestic space to understand the construction of the territory is a first exercise within a broader and deeper geographical practice, which requires the contribution of perspectives with a gender perspective, from socio-environmental conflicts and resistance in defending the territory, where experiences and voices of those who inhabit these spaces are retaken and are part of this biocultural continuity of the Yucatán Peninsula.

Notes

1 Some examples include for the territory, the National Program for the Certification of Ejidal Rights and Urban Lots-PROCEDE (1993) and the North American Free Trade Agreement-NAFTA (1994), and for the homesteads, the use of the Natural Disasters Fund-FONDEN, after Hurricane Isidore (2002), and the offer of credits to build Maya-style houses for tourism purposes, but not for living in them (Cabrera Pacheco, 2017).
2 Corn drink served in Jícaras.
3 Ceremony related to bees, to thank the honey harvest (Rosales and Rubio, 2010).
4 Thanksgiving ceremony after harvest (Terán and Rasmussen, 2009).
5 Thick broth made from corn dough.
6 Knead.
7 Rain request ceremony, when the planting is ready (Terán and Rasmussen, 2009).
8 Traditional healer or Maya priest who performs agricultural ceremonies.
9 As part of the Maya Women in Defence of Seeds Panel Discussion, organised by the Casa Colibrí Cultural and Human Rights Centre on 31/01/2021.

Bibliography

Aké Gómez, A., Jiménez-Osornio, J., and Ruenes-Morales, M. (1999). El Solar maya. En: P. Chico (Ed.), *Atlas de Procesos Territoriales de Yucatán* (pp. 236–245). UADY.

Argumedo, A. (n.d.) *Territorios bioculturales indígenas: Una propuesta para la protección de territorios indígenas y el Buen Vivir*. Asociación ANDES. http://www.internationalfunders.org/documents/TerritoriosBioculturalesIndigenas.pdf

Barbosa, L. (2021). De las mujeres como energía vital y las reverberaciones de la lucha en defensa de los territorios y de los comunes en América Latina. En: A. Calderón Cisneros, M. Olivera Bustamante, and M. Arellano Nucamendi (Eds.), *Territorios para la vida. Mujeres en defensa de sus bienes naturales y por la sostenibilidad de la vida* (pp. 23–55). UNICACH.

Bezaury Creel, J., Graf Montero, S., Barclay Briseño, K., de la Maza Hernández, R., Machado Macías, S., Rodríguez Martínez, E., Rojas González, S., and Ruíz Barranco, H. (2015). *Los paisajes bioculturales, un instrumento para el desarrollo rural y la conservación del patrimonio natural y cultural*. CONANP - Agencia Francesa de Desarrollo.

Boege, E. (2008). *El patrimonio biocultural de los pueblos indígenas de México: Hacia la conservación in situ de la biodiversidad y agrodiversidad en los territorios indígenas*. INAH; CDI.

Boege, E. (2014). Las regiones bioculturales de México, *La Jornada del Campo*, 79, 3.

Cabrera Pacheco, A. (2014). Estrategias de sustentabilidad en el Solar maya yucateco en Mérida, México, *GeoGraphos*, 5, 1–32.

Cabrera Pacheco, A. (2017). Primitive accumulation in indigenous Mexico: The contested transformations of the Maya Solar of Yucatán, *City*, 21(3–4), 503–519.

Calderón, A., and Santiz, C. (2021). La defensa del territorio desde la realidad cotidiana de las mujeres indígenas: Apuestas y contradicciones. En: A. Calderón, M. Olivera, and M. Arellano (Eds.), *Territorios para la vida. Mujeres en defensa de sus bienes naturales y por la sostenibilidad de la vida* (1a., 115–143). UNICACH.

Carrasco, N. (2020). Miradas decoloniales, interculturales y ecología política en la gobernanza de territorios, *Utopía y Praxis Latinoamericana*, 25(88), 34–40.

Colectivo Suumil Mookt'an. (2022, febrero 25). *Presentación Folleto Suumil—Solar Maya* [Reunión en Zoom].

Collignon, B. (2010). De las virtudes de los espacios domésticos para la geografía humana. En: A. Lindón and D. Hiernaux (Eds.), *Los giros de la Geografía Humana: Desafíos y horizontes* (pp. 201–216). UAM.

Correa Navarro, P. (1997). La agricultura de Solar en la zona henequenera yucateca. *Su evolución y sus posibilidades de mejoramiento productivo [Tesis de maestría]*. Universidad Autónoma Chapingo.
Duarte Duarte, A. (2014). Las autonomías de los pueblos mayas de Yucatán y su silencio ante las políticas de asimilación y la legislación de sus derechos, *Pueblos y fronteras digital*, 8(16), 256–281.
Duarte Duarte, A. (2018). K'ax: Modos de Habitar y Pervivencia Cultural del Pueblo Maya, *Gremium*, 5(10).
Dussel, E. (1994). 1492. El encubrimiento del otro: Hacia el origen del mito de la modernidad. UMSA; Plural Editores.
Dzib Hau, R. (2018). *Los significados otorgados a la cocina tradicional por hombres y mujeres de tres grupos domésticos macehuales de la comunidad de Huay Max, Quintana Roo [Tesis de maestría]*. El Colegio de la Frontera Sur.
Ek Cohuo, G. (2020). Foro Virtual "Para una sana nutrición en la Península de Yucatán, ¿Qué estamos comiendo?"
Escobar, A. (2015). Territorios de diferencia: La ontología política de los "derechos al territorio". *Desenvolvimento e Meio Ambiente*, 35.
Estrada Lugo, E., Bello Baltazar, E., and Serralta Peraza, L. (1998). Dimensiones de la etnobotánica: El Solar maya como espacio social. En: J. Cuevas, E. Cedillo, A. Muñoz, and P. Vera (Eds.), *Lecturas en Etnobotánica* (pp. 457–474). Universidad Autónoma Chapingo.
Flores, A., and Deniau, Y. (2019). *El megaproyecto para la península de Yucatán*. GeoComunes/Consejo Civil Mexicano para la Silvicultura Sostenible.
García de Miguel, J. (2000). *Etnobotánica Maya: Origen y evolución de los huertos familiares de la Península de Yucatán, México*. Universidad de Córdoba.
González, C., Urrutia, A., Alonso-Fernández, C., Mora, E., Castro Campero, L., García, L., Ramos, I., Hernández, B., and Benítez, M. (2021). Agricultura, biodiversidad y diversidad cultural en paisajes campesinos: Una relación de mutua determinación. En: M. Benítez, T. Rivera-Núñez, and L. García-Barrios (Eds.), *Agroecología y sistemas complejos. Planteamientos epistémicos, casos de estudio y enfoques metodológicos* (pp. 51–74). CopIt-arXives and SOCLA–México.
Gudynas, E. (2011). Buen Vivir: Germinando alternativas al desarrollo, *América Latina en Movimiento*, 462, 1–20.
Gudynas, E., and Acosta, A. (2011). La renovación de la crítica al desarrollo y el Buen Vivir como alternativa, *Utopía y Praxis Latinoamericana*, 16(53), 71–83.
Haesbaert, R. (2020). Territory/ies from a Latin American Perspective (L. Mason-Deese, Trad.), *Journal of Latin American Geography*, 19(1), 258–268.
Halvorsen, S. (2019). Decolonising territory: Dialogues with Latin American knowledges and grassroots strategies, *Progress in Human Geography*, 43(5), 790–814.
Hernández Sánchez, M. (2010). Cambios y Continuidades en los Solares Mayas Yucatecos. *Un Análisis Intergeneracional de su Configuración Espacial en Dos Comunidades del Sur de Yucatán [Tesis de maestría]*. Centro de Investigación y de Estudios Avanzados del Instituto Politécnico Nacional.
Heyl, B. (2001). Ethonographic Interviewing. En: P. Atkinson, A. Coffey, S. Delamont, J. Lofland, and L. Lofland (Eds.), *Handbook of Ethnography* (pp. 369–383). Sage Publications.
Huanacuni Mamani, F. (2010). *Buen Vivir/Vivir Bien: Filosofía, políticas, estrategias y experiencias regionales andinas*. Coordinadora Andina de Organizaciones Indígenas.
INEGI. (2020). Censo Población y Vivienda 2020. Censo de Población y Vivienda 2020.
Jiménez-Osornio, J., Zarco, M., Lendechy, Á., and Becerril-García, J. (2015). Los Solares: Una oportunidad para contribuir a la seguridad alimentaria, mitigación y cambio climático en Yucatán. En: R. Canto and M. Zarco (Eds.), *Extensión y responsabilidad social: Los proyectos sociales en comunidades de aprendizaje implementados en la Universidad Autónoma de Yucatán* (pp. 237–264). Ediciones de la UADY.

Jordan, S., and Yeomans, D. (1995). Critical Ethnography: Problems in Contemporary Theory and Practice, *British Journal of Sociology of Education*, 16(3), 389–408.
Lope-Alzina, D. (2014). Una red comunal de acceso a alimentos: El huerto familiar como principal proveedor de productos para intercambio en una comunidad Maya-Yucateca, *Gaia Scientia*, 8(2), 199–215.
López Barreto, M., Hernández Cueva, F., and Becerril-García, J. (2018). El patrimonio biocultural maya-yucateco desde la perspectiva de la ecología política: El caso del huerto familiar en Chimay, *Journal of Political Ecology*, 25(1), 312.
López Córdova, D., and Marañón Pimentel, B. (2013). *Racionalidades y prácticas socioproductivas alternativas para el Buen Vivir*. UNAM.
López Sandoval, M., Robertsdotter, A., and Paredes, M. (2017). Space, Power, and Locality: The Contemporary Use of Territorio in Latin American Geography, *Journal of Latin American Geography*, 16(1), 43–67.
López Valentín, R., Rosset, P., Zamora Lomelí, C., Giraldo Palacio, O., and González Santiago, M. (2020). Identidad y espiritualidad maya en la Escuela de Agricultura Ecológica U Yits Ka'an en Maní, Yucatán, México, *Revista Práxis Educacional*, 16(39), 450–472.
Macías López, R. (2021). *Usos de la tierra en los territorios bioculturales: El caso de Metzabok, en la Selva Lacandona, Chiapas, México [Tesis de maestría]*. Universidad Autónoma Chapingo.
Maffi, L. (2018). Biocultural Diversity. En: H. Callan (Ed.), *The International Encyclopedia of Anthropology* (pp. 1–14). Wiley.
Medeiros, R. (2008). Território, espaço de identidade. En: M. Saquet and E. Sposito (Eds.), *Territórios e territorialidades: Teorias, processos e conflitos*(pp. 217–228). UNESP.
Mignolo, W. (2002). The Geopolitics of Knowledge and the Colonial Difference, *The South Atlantic Quarterly*, 101(1), 57–96.
Morales Barragán, F. (2019). Paisaje biocultural: Participación vs gestión asociada del territorio. En: *Impactos ambientales, gestión de recursos naturales y turismo en el desarrollo regional: Vol. II* (pp. 214–226). UNAM y AMECIDER.
Moreno-Calles, A., Toledo, V., and Casas, A. (2013). Los sistemas agroforestales tradicionales de México: Una aproximación biocultural, *Botanical Sciences*, 91(4), 375–398.
Nigh, R., and Ford, A. (2019). *El Jardín Forestal Maya: Ocho Milenios de Cultivo Sostenido de los Bosques Tropicales*. Fray Bartolomé de Las Casas A.C.
Orellana Lanza, R. (2015). Cambio climático en la Península de Yucatán (Estrategia de cambio climático de la Península de Yucatán). http://www.ccpy.gob.mx/cambio-climatico/peninsula-yucatan.php
Otzen, T., and Manterola, C. (2017). Técnicas de Muestreo sobre una Población a Estudio, *International Journal of Morphology*, 35(1), 227–232.
Pérez Ruiz, M. (2017). Las muchachas mayas de Yaxcabá, Yucatán, *LiminaR Estudios Sociales y Humanísticos*, 15(1), 58–81.
Pérez Ruiz, M. (2018). La milpa como patrimonio biocultural. En: E. Peña, L. Hernández, and J. Machuca (Eds.), *Biodiversidad, patrimonio y cocina: Procesos bioculturales sobre alimentación-nutrición* (pp. 215–236). Secretaría de Cultura, INAH.
Pérez Salas, G. (2020). Saberes indígenas: El poder político/espacial/simbólico contra el sistema-mundo capitalista moderno/colonial/patriarcal, *Boletín Geocrítica Latinoamericana*, 4, 17–20.
Quintal, E., Bastarrachea, J., Briceño, F., Medina, M., Petrich, R., Rejón, L., Repetto, B., and Rosales, M. (2003). Solares, rumbos y pueblos: Organización social de los mayas peninsulares. En: S. Millán and J. Valle (Eds.), *La comunidad sin límites. La estructura social y comunitaria de los pueblos indígenas de México* (Vol. 1, pp. 291–399). INAH.

Ribeiro, B., and Ponte, V. (2020). "A nossa briga mesmo é a terra, prioritária": Saberes tradicionais, saúde e territorialidade entre os Tembé do Guamá (Terra Indígena Alto Rio Guamá – Pará, Brasil), *Boletín Geocrítica Latinoamericana*, 4, 30–40.

Rosado-May, F., and Poot, H. (2020). Cosmovisión Maya reflejada en palabras y conceptos relacionados con desarrollo sostenible, ecología y agroecología, *DasQuestões*, 10(1), 33–48.

Rosales, M., and Rubio, A. (2010). Apicultura y organizaciones de apicultores entre los mayas de Yucatán, *Estudios de Cultura Maya*, 35, 163–186.

Sañudo Vélez, L. (2013). La casa como territorio. Una nueva epistemología sobre el hábitat humano y su lugar doméstico, *Iconofacto*, 9(12), 214–231.

Saquet, M. (2008). Por uma abordagem territorial. En: M. Saquet and E. Sposito (Eds.), *Territórios e territorialidades: Teorias, processos e conflitos*(pp. 73–94). UNESP.

Schmitter-Soto, J., Comín, F., Escobar-Briones, E., Herrera-Silveira, J., Alcocer, J., Suárez-Morales, E., Elías-Gutiérrez, M., Díaz-Arce, V., Marín, L., and Steinich, B. (2002). Hydrogeochemical and Biological Characteristics of Cenotes in the Yucatan Peninsula (SE Mexico), *Hydrobiologia*, 467(1–3), 215–228.

Sinco Ramos, G. (2015). *Análisis de la propuesta de educación ambiental y cultural elaborada por Kaxil Kiuic A.C. para la Región Puuc en Yucatán, México [Informe Preliminar para Kaxil Kiuic A.C.]*. CATIE.

Sultana, F. (2007). Reflexivity, Positionality and Participatory Ethics: Negotiating Fieldwork Dilemmas in International Research, *ACME: An International E-Journal for Critical Geographies*, 6(3), 374–385.

Svampa, M. (2012). Pensar el desarrollo desde América Latina. En: G. Massuh (Ed.), *Renunciar al bien común. Extractivismo y (pos)desarrollo en América Latina* (pp. 17–58). Editorial Mardulce.

Terán, S., and Rasmussen, C. (2009). *La milpa de los mayas: La agricultura de los mayas prehispánicos y actuales en el noreste de Yucatán (2a.)*. UNAM; CIESAS; UdO.

Toledo, V., and Barrera-Bassols, N. (2008a). *La memoria biocultural*. Icaria.

Toledo, V., and Barrera-Bassols, N. (2008b). Uso múltiple y biodiversidad entre los mayas yucatecos (México). 33, 345–352.

Toledo, V., Barrera-Bassols, N., and Boege, E. (2019). *¿Qué es el Diversidad Biocultural?* UNAM.

Toledo, V., Boege, E., and Barrera-Bassols, N. (2014). The Biocultural Heritage of Mexico: A Case Study. En: L. Maffi and O. Dilts (Eds.), *Biocultural Diversity Toolkit Volume 1—Introduction to Biocultural Diversity* (Vol. 1, pp. 22–31). Terralingua.

Torres-Mazuera, G. (2018). Nosotros decimos ma': La lucha contra la soya transgénica y la rearticulación de la identidad maya en la Península de Yucatán, *The Journal of Latin American and Caribbean Anthropology*, 23(2), 262–280.

Trinh, M. (1997). Not you/Like you: Post-colonial Women and the Interlocking Questions of Identity and Difference. En: Dangerous Liasons. *Gender, Nation, and Postcolonial Perspectives* (pp. 415–419). University of Minnesota Press.

Vásquez-Dávila, M., and Lope-Alzina, D. (2012). Manejo y Conservación de la agrodiversidad y biodiversidad en huertos familiares indígenas de Oaxaca, México: Un enfoque biocultural. *En Los huertos familiares en Mesoamérica* (pp. 280–308). UADY.

Velázquez Solís, A. (2012). *De prácticas y saberes entre la milpa y el Solar. Género, Cosmovisión y Medio Ambiente en Yaxcabá, Yucatán. [Tesis de maestría]*. Centro de Investigaciones y Estudios Superiores en Antropología Social.

Wejebe Shanahan, M., and Rodríguez Pavón, J. (2014). Transformaciones socioespaciales e identidad local: Proyectos inmobiliarios en Cholul y reserva ecológica de San José Tzal. En: *Crecimiento urbano y cambio social: Escenarios de transformación de la zona metropolitana de Mérida* (pp. 391–418). UNAM.

9 Regional cooperation as local development agendas

Coffee Cultural Landscape (Colombia) and Coopeumo (Chile)

Diana Morales

Introduction

The purpose of this chapter is to explain how regional cooperation strategies respond to the socio-economic and cultural composition of territories, exerting influence on local development agendas. The findings stem from a comparative case study of the Coffee Cultural Landscape (PCC), located in the Colombian Coffee Region, and the Peumo Farmer Cooperative (Coopeumo), located in the Sixth Region of Chile, officially known as the Libertador General Bernardo O'Higgins Region.

Both the PCC and Coopeumo are defined, for the purpose of this document, as alternative regional cooperation processes capable of influencing local and regional development agendas in their respective regions. This chapter addresses the research question: how do regional cooperation processes reflect territorial configurations, and what effect do they have on local development? Among the findings considered most relevant are, first, the role that historical, social, and economic contexts play in the creation of cooperation processes; the form they take; and the actors involved. Second, regional cooperation processes reflect both the socio-economic and cultural elements, as well as the ineffectiveness of administrative boundaries to facilitate local development processes. Third, regional cooperation is one of several forms of negotiating local and regional development agendas, used to address some of the problems caused by top-down policies.

This document is divided into five sections. The second section defines regional cooperation and local development. The third section presents the methodology and case studies, emphasising on the historical, social, and economic elements that have most influenced the emergence and evolution of the PCC and Coopeumo. The fourth section explains the influence of the PCC and Coopeumo on the local and regional development agenda. The chapter ends with the conclusions in the fifth section.

DOI: 10.4324/9781032650241-11

Regional cooperation and local development

Regional cooperation is a phenomenon studied by different disciplines. In general, it is recognised that regional cooperation consists of agreements between different actors seeking the development and wellbeing of a community. This wellbeing is often reflected in income generation, provision of public services, production efficiency, or protection and conservation of culture or the environment (Quintero-López, 2006; Rodríguez-Oreggia and Gutiérrez, 2006; Spicer, 2015). However, definitions can vary according to the discipline looking at them. Below, regional cooperation is explained according to different approaches.

Regional cooperation in public administration studies

Regional cooperation is defined as a set of agreements between local or regional governments with other public authorities or private organisations (Hulst et al., 2009). These agreements are usually implemented in municipalities and localities with geographical proximity that share at least one common problem, typically related to the provision of public services (Citroni, Lippi, and Profeti, 2013). These are agreements that are executed to provide one or more specific functions, which may or may not alter the spatial composition of territories and depend on clearly pre-defined administrative and governmental functions (Hophmayer-Tokich, 2008). Table 9.1 summarises the most common forms of regional cooperation studied by public administration studies.

Table 9.1 Types of regional cooperation in public administration

Criteria	*Types*
Objectives	Service delivery or policy coordination Single or multi-purpose
Actors involved	Horizontal (local governments only) Vertical (other levels of government or private actors)
Level of the initiative and local governments` autonomy	Voluntary or bottom-up Induced or top-down
Formalisation	Contracts Standing organisations
New administrative units	Mergers Metropolitan areas Polycentric regions

Source: Morales-Arcila, 2018

It has been argued that regional cooperation depends on transaction costs being lower than the benefits created by the economies of scale sought to be established with the agreements (Feiock, 2006, 2007). Consequently, regional cooperation occurs only if the expected benefits outweigh the costs of negotiation, coordination, monitoring, and execution of the agreements (Gillette, 2005). Once transaction costs have been evaluated, the creation of agreements depends on five variables (Spicer, 2015): first, there must be interaction and networks that create trust and reciprocity. Second, the group composition must allow coordination, management, and distribution of benefits and commitments. The larger the group, the less likely there is to be cooperation and the agreement maintained. Third, there must be geographical proximity. Cooperation occurs more easily among actors who are closer to each other. Fourth, there must be symmetry in power; asymmetric power among actors can generate coercive cooperation relationships rather than voluntary ones. Fifth, there must be political leadership. Typically, local governments are responsible for initiating and formalising agreements.

While transaction costs and economies of scale explain the establishment of cooperation agreements at the organisational level (local or regional governments), institutionalism has been responsible for explaining the incentives that allow cooperation within the framework of interaction between actors and institutions (North, 1998; Hulst et al., 2009). It is argued that cooperation is influenced by the behaviour of those involved in cooperation schemes, which in turn is influenced by a set of objectives, interests, and preferences that interact in an institutional environment. In other words, regional cooperation also depends on how actors and the institutions framing them interact. The institutional environment includes, first, the formal structure of the state, its administrative organisations, and the distribution of responsibilities among different levels of government; second, administrative culture, including values, norms, informal rules, and traditions related to the state, its political organisation, and its public administration; and, finally, legislation and incentive structures that are specifically related to cooperation (Hulst et al., 2009).

Public administration studies provide a framework for analysing different forms of regional cooperation and understanding why individuals and organisations decide to create agreements with each other. However, debates on models of local and regional development, as well as the spatial composition of territories, are absent. Therefore, it is necessary to turn to geography and development studies.

Regional cooperation in geography studies

Much of geography studies have focused on studying regional cooperation as a strategy to adapt to the global economy and processes of decentralisation of power from the National State (Perkmann, 2007; Nelles and Durand, 2014). The debate has focused on issues of scale and governance, the expansion of metropolitan areas, and the fragmentation of municipalities in the United States (Feiock, 2005; Oakerson, 2007) and the emergence of cross-border regions in Europe (Perkmann, 2002, 2003; Nelles and Durand, 2014). These processes are usually analysed from the perspective of rescaling regions in response to the global economy, the influence of transnational organisations such as the European Union, and decentralisation processes (Brenner, 2003; Egermann, 2009).

Recognising metropolitan governance and cross-border cooperation has contributed to broadening the understanding of territories beyond jurisdictional borders. It also highlights the qualitative re-composition of the state, by recognising the creation of institutional spaces that become forms of interdependent and overlapping territorial organisation (MacLeod, 2001). Despite advances in recognising territories beyond their administrative boundaries, the focus on the global north makes it difficult to fully apply these categories to the case studies. Therefore, these advances can be complemented with studies on development, which have focused on other forms of cooperation between regional actors, alternative regional cooperation forms emerging from the local scale in response to patterns of exclusion and inequality (Whyte, 1995; Larner and Craig, 2005; Gibson-Graham, 2008, 2011).

From a post-development perspective, regional cooperation is related to non-capitalist forms of social partnership that create economies focused on social benefits rather than capital accumulation (Gibson-Graham, 2008). Contexts of exclusion, unequal economic growth, and unemployment, exacerbated by the failures of capitalist and neoliberal policies, became fertile ground for the emergence of alternative economies from the local level (Sarria, 2002). These cooperation strategies encompass a wide variety of local initiatives such as community projects, social movements, neighbourhood organisations, and the most common form, worker or producer cooperatives (Chatterton and Gordon, 2004; Perreault, 2006; Escobar, 2010). Cooperatives are defined as organisations in which property rights and governance control are shared among stakeholders rather than investors and are often recognised as alternatives to conventional economic models that develop in a context of economic inequality and exclusion (Michie et al., 2017).

Cooperatives are not usually accounted for in the literature on regional cooperation but in studies on solidarity economy, collective action, and post-development. However, their inclusion here becomes relevant insofar as they are strategies of joint work at the local level capable of impacting local and regional development (Morales-Arcila, 2018). Non-capitalist forms of economy, based on cooperative work involving private actors, local authorities, and universities, coexist with traditional economic dynamics, improving welfare and producing social benefits (Gibson-Graham, 2011; Whyte, 1995). In other words, regional cooperation processes inspired by a post-development background do not necessarily reject capitalist economies but recognise the need to acknowledge the different forms of economic activity that exist in a territory (Gibson-Graham, 2006).

Regional cooperation and local development

Understanding development as a bottom-up process is fundamental to explaining regional cooperation processes and their effect on local development. The concept of local and regional development has a long theoretical tradition, from classical economics, neoclassical, Keynesian, and Marxist theories, to more holistic approaches inspired by post-development and anti-capitalist theories (Pike et al., 2011). More recently, local and regional development has been associated with innovation, knowledge, and change. These approaches pay special attention to the links between economic action and sociocultural practices at the local-regional level, for example, theories of competitive advantage and cluster theories. In general, it can be said that local development is understood as the improvement of the locality or region's capacity to produce, absorb, and use innovations and knowledge and thus generate and retain value (Mackinnon, Cumbers, and Chapman, 2002).

On the other hand, post-development theories question the discourse and paradigms of development and modernity. It is argued that dominant development obstructs people's ability to shape their own behaviour and reproduces social and cultural domination through the homogeneous application of Westernised values (Escobar, 1995). Furthermore, it is argued that economic development theories are incompatible with ecological concerns and have widened the gap between rich and poor countries (Ziai, 2007). Recent contributions from post-development theorists focus on what is called alternatives to development, for example, grassroots movements, community projects, indigenous movements, and environmental actions that challenge traditional understandings of the economy and neoliberalism (Chatterton and Gordon, 2004; Ziai, 2007; Escobar, 2010; Asher and Wainwright, 2019). The post-developmentalist approach to local and regional development focuses on social, cultural, and human issues, rather than on competitiveness and successful incorporation into the global productive system, recognising localities, regions, and communities as the axis of their own development (Gibson-Graham, 2011).

A local and regional approach to development seeks to explain development in relation to territories, providing context-based solutions. However, theories of local and regional development cannot offer consensus on how to solve development problems. None of the proposed approaches, whether agglomeration theories, innovation, or community projects, are necessarily exclusive of each other. Experience has shown that local and regional development cannot be achieved by following a single set of tools, that the definition of development varies over time and space, and that each territory has different priorities, needs, and characteristics that lead to different processes and outcomes (Pike, Rodríguez-Pose, and Tomaney, 2007). This is why studying regional cooperation processes is relevant, as they can provide clues as to what the priorities, desires, and potentialities of the territories are (Morales, 2020).

Methodology and case studies

This chapter is part of a broader research effort aimed at explaining regional cooperation processes and their territorial impact (see Morales-Arcila, 2018; Morales, 2020, 2021). This research was based on a comparative case study using qualitative methods. This research uses both secondary and primary data. Secondary data come from sources such as reports from international organisations like the United Nations, the Organization for Economic Cooperation and Development (OECD), and the Food and Agriculture Organization of the United Nations (FAO). Legislation and reports from government entities regarding decentralisation policies, norms for regional cooperation, and local development strategies are also utilised. As for primary data, information was obtained from 37 interviews conducted in the Coffee Region (19 interviews during 2015) and the O'Higgins region (18 interviews during 2016). Table 9.2 summarises the categories of interviewees.

Table 9.2 List and description of interviewees

Category	*Description*
Professionals from the public sector, local level (9 interviews)	Interviews of local government representatives illustrated the role of the local governments in the cases; how they are related to the national level, decision-making processes, and rationales for implementing a cooperative process
Professionals from the public sector, national level (5 interviews)	Professionals from the national level were involved in the cases. These interviews illustrated the relationship between the national and local levels, and the influence of the national level on regional cooperation
Private sector (9 interviews including a few *campesinos*)	Representatives from the most salient economic activities that illustrated the rationales and outcomes of cooperation within each sector and its participation in the process
Leaders and active participants of regional cooperation processes (12 interviews including a few *campesinos*)	Promoters and professionals who provided information about the design and implementation process, including experts who provided a critical perspective
Civic sector (2 interviews)	Organised institutions were not necessarily part of the cases but were impacted by them

Fuente Morales-Arcila, 2018

Coffee Cultural Landscape

The PCC covers an area of 141,120 hectares and is declared a UNESCO World Heritage Site under the category of Cultural Landscape. This declaration recognises the unique characteristics derived from the interaction between the territory, its inhabitants, and its main economic activity, highlighting the cultural, institutional, and natural features of the region related to coffee production. Its objective is the protection, conservation, and rehabilitation of the cultural and natural landscape (PCC, 2009; 2010). The PCC recognises the close link between the territory, its culture, and its economy, but it does not grant any type of jurisdictional or administrative power.

The PCC, located in the area known as the Coffee Region, consists of a series of municipalities and rural areas from the departments of Caldas, Quindío, Risaralda, and the northern part of Valle Del Cauca. The Coffee Region is not a legally recognised region, but it is often referred to as one, thanks to its shared historical and cultural roots. The region's economy has depended on agricultural production, particularly coffee, making it especially vulnerable to fluctuations in international markets (Toro-Zuluaga, 2004). Due to protectionist policies and production and purchase agreements contained in the International Coffee Agreement, the region enjoyed a period of economic prosperity for much of the 20th century until the late 1980s. During this period, the Coffee Region was considered an example of regional development in Colombia, especially in rural development. Investments in rural and social infrastructure, however, were the responsibility of the National Federation of Coffee Growers, which for a time functioned as a quasi-state entity in the region, taking charge of investments that would normally be the responsibility of the state (PNUD, 2004; Toro-Zuluaga, 2004).

Once the International Coffee Agreement was dissolved in 1989, coinciding with the Colombian economy's neoliberalisation, the region entered a period of economic stagnation from which it has not yet emerged (PNUD, 2004). In fact, social and economic conditions in the region declined to such an extent that the period 1992–2003 is referred to as the lost decade by the local academia (Arango-Gaviria, 2008). In January 1999, an earthquake with its epicentre in the region caused serious human, infrastructure, and economic losses, exacerbating social problems, inequality, unemployment, and internal migration. Today, the Coffee Region has shown slow adaptation and little resilience to the economic changes brought about by neoliberal reforms (Toro-Zuluaga, 2004; Arango-Gaviria, 2008), with high unemployment and informality rates, and transitioning towards an economy based on services, especially tourism services (Morales-Arcila, 2018).

The PCC is not usually understood as an example of regional cooperation, as it involves a series of agreements, commitments, and tasks carried out by a group of actors, mostly from the academic and private sectors in coordination with other actors at the local and national levels, which does not fit into or materialise as a territorial or administrative unit but rather as a recognition (UNESCO World Heritage Site) and a regional brand. However, its temporality (the process began in 1995 and continues to the date of publication of this book), the type of actors it brings together (public, private, and academic actors at the local, regional, and national levels), and its objectives (promoting an agenda for the development and conservation of landscape and cultural attributes) make it a process of regional cooperation with peculiar characteristics.

The process began as an initiative of a group of local academics seeking to highlight the natural and cultural attributes of one municipality (unlike the 47 that are now part of the PCC), to revitalise and diversify its economy through tourism (Morales-Arcila, 2018). Obtaining international recognition was the most viable option, as it would generate the necessary incentives to attract investment and update and protect land use. Applying to UNESCO required the national government's approval, which requested to extend the project to the whole region (interviews; PCC, 2009; 2010). This is how the project took on a regional scope. From 1995 to 2011, the year the PCC was included in the UNESCO World Heritage List, more actors from the public and private sectors were involved through working groups, the management and administration scheme of the project was designed, and the management plan of the PCC was written and approved (interviews; PCC, 2009, 2010). PCC is organised under the principles of economic and social development, ownership and belonging, and environmental sustainability, meaning that the activities and projects developed within its framework must contribute to strengthening these aspects in the territory. These strategies include promoting traditional good practices in coffee production, investing in rural infrastructure, encouraging democratic processes within the National Federation of Coffee Growers, and promoting regional alliances between different local governments, among others (PCC, 2009).

Peumo farmers' cooperative (Coopeumo)

Coopeumo is a farmers' cooperative with around 360 members, mostly producers of fruits, vegetables, and corn on small plots averaging 12 hectares. The cooperative operates in four municipalities covering 21% of the rural population of the region. It is located in the Sixth Region of Chile, a single political-administrative territory housing three provinces and 33 municipalities. Its economy depends on copper extraction and agricultural activities primarily aimed at export, making it vulnerable to fluctuations in prices in international markets. The region has more industrial development than the Coffee Region but is limited to a few economic sectors such as food production and packaging (Ortega-Melo, 2006).

Chile's history is clearly divided, before and after the dictatorship, which began in 1973 and lasted until 1990. During this period, radical economic reforms were introduced, transitioning from an economy with an interventionist state and ownership of certain sectors such as copper to a neoliberal economy. Chile served as a neoliberal laboratory where privatisation and free market policies were rapidly implemented with the support of a repressive and violent government (Ostry et al., 2016; Rehner, Baeza, & Barton, 2016). These reforms had a strong impact on the region; social transformations such as the agrarian reform, which began in 1964 in response to social protests over labour and social precarity and aimed to grant land ownership to non-landowning peasants (who represented a large part of the region's population at the time), were halted (Morales-Arcila, 2018). Although copper exports and some agricultural products have increased, thanks to neoliberal policies, in O'Higgins, it has been the large producers and owners of extensive land who have benefited the most from this economic model, while many small-scale farmers and other producers have had to face unsustainable competition conditions, increased demands for quality, innovation, and commercialisation, leaving them out of the regional economy (FAO, 2012b; interviews). In February 2010, an earthquake followed by a tsunami, with its epicentre on the coast near central Chile, left the region with severe material losses, especially in rural areas.

Coopeumo was founded in 1969 as part of the agrarian reform process, in response to the lack of inputs and working capital that peasants received with the land awarded to them. It has evolved from being a small cooperative in the municipality of Peumo (where its main offices are located today) to being an inter-municipal cooperative. It survived the years of dictatorship with the support of international organisations and the Catholic Church and now consolidates itself as an organisation dedicated to improving the quality of life of its members, their families, and the communities where they live (interviews, FAO, 2012a). Coopeumo maintains a balance between its identity as a capitalist organisation seeking profits and its identity as a social organisation seeking social welfare and rural development. Coopeumo sells agricultural products, works to find national and international markets, provides technical services, and grants low-interest loans, while offering scholarships to outstanding students from rural schools, providing internet service to remote rural schools, or serving as an intermediary for the government to manage reconstruction resources for those affected by the 2010 earthquake.

In terms of its participation in public regional life, the cooperative and its founding members have played a fundamental role in regional history, for example, as active participants in the protests that led to the agrarian reform of the 1970s or participating in local politics. Coopeumo interacts with the national government through funding calls, technical support, and training offered by public institutions, and with the regional government through political debates. Coopeumo members and its administrative team firmly believe that through cooperative work, farmers can take advantage of the policies of free market and economic globalisation (Morales-Arcila, 2018).

Building territories through cooperation

Regional cooperation is a contextual process influenced by history, economy, and politics. It brings together independent actors, impacting local and regional development. For PCC and Coopeumo, cooperation arises from the need to address persistent issues of unequal development and respond to state inefficiency and dissatisfaction with policies that disregard local contexts (Morales, 2018). It is built between agents and territories with shared socio-economic and cultural characteristics, rendering administrative borders irrelevant.

Both PCC and Coopeumo recognise that territories are composed of connections that go beyond jurisdictional boundaries. The territory in which they have influence is delimited not by contained administrative divisions, but by a series of economic, social, and cultural characteristics common to the space and its inhabitants. PCC encompasses areas with socio-economic, natural, and cultural characteristics unique to those territories (Morales, 2020; Gaviria Rios, 2020). Coopeumo covers an area inhabited by small-scale farmers facing competition conditions with large agro-industries difficult to overcome individually, which are also connected by a history of cooperativism and social activism. The cases reflect how the territories in which they have influence are socially constructed. However, for PCC, this territorial flexibility has brought problems when designing and managing resources that require public approval and financing, as, generally, legislation does not allow investments beyond administrative boundaries. On the contrary, when it comes to participating in public funding, Coopeumo has the advantage of being able to present itself as an organisation from the solidarity sector.

The territoriality of PCC and Coopeumo goes beyond geographical proximity. In the case of PCC, the work of other entities such as the National Federation of Coffee Growers, Chambers of Commerce, and Ministries has been fundamental in building the management plan that now serves as a roadmap. In the case of Coopeumo, its interaction with similar organisations in other countries has served to open markets and adapt to the economic conditions of globalisation, and agreements with academia have allowed it to invest in agricultural innovation.

Uneven local development

Uneven development is the primary driver behind PCC and Coopeumo. Those involved in these initiatives emphasise the potential of cooperative work to solve local and regional problems where the state has been inefficient. The rural populations in the Coffee Region and O'Higgins, and more broadly in Colombia and Chile, have historically faced marginalisation and high rates of poverty, violence, and inequality. These persistent issues, exacerbated by patterns of violence, neoliberal economic policies, excessive centralism, financial limitations, and unequal institutional capacities, necessitate cooperation. Thus, cooperation is not only about surviving economic globalisation but also about addressing historical problems (Morales-Arcila, 2018). This results in complex regional cooperation schemes with multiple objectives aimed at solving problems beyond the capacity of the involved actors.

Regional cooperation processes emerge as alternatives to meet unmet needs. PCC and Coopeumo are innovative initiatives seeking to protect and manage the landscape, local economy, and culture, challenging national policies. PCC aims to propose a local and sustainable development agenda, Coopeumo seeks to solve issues of low income and access to means of production for peasants. These strategies highlight the inefficiency of 'self-correcting' market mechanisms and demonstrate the need to listen to local voices in deciding local and regional development strategies. They also underscore that local and regional development is a continuous negotiation among different actors, scales, and models, with local actors demanding a more active role.

Local development agendas

Through PCC and Coopeumo, local concerns such as social wellbeing, environmental sustainability and inequality gained attention in the local development agendas. This will be expanded below.

Local development and social wellbeing

For both PCC and Coopeumo, social wellbeing plays a fundamental role in defining their strategies. In both cases, discussions about housing, income, entrepreneurship, health, and education are part of their agendas, while creating participatory spaces to discuss the elements that can improve people's wellbeing and quality of life.

In the case of PCC, contributions to local development and social wellbeing are evident in its efforts to bring discussions about rural development models to the public agenda. This includes involving a greater number of actors in debates and strengthening the sense of belonging among landscape inhabitants, making PCC a regional brand that must be preserved by all residents, not just those directly involved in its administration. PCC has produced numerous publications to promote the project and its programmes, while local universities incorporate relevant PCC topics into their academic programmes and extension activities.

Coopeumo contributes to social wellbeing through programmes designed to directly impact the quality of life of its members, their families, and their communities. They focus on addressing the most urgent or valuable needs expressed by members. Coopeumo also aids local development by enabling farmers to participate in and benefit from the regional economy, providing technical assistance services, and granting access to shared storage centres that meet international standards, facilitating the export of stored products.

Local and sustainable development

The debate about development models goes beyond discussions on social welfare and quality of life. Concerns for local and sustainable development are also part of the PCC and Coopeumo's agenda. The discussions revolve around environmentally friendly agricultural production methods, conservation of water sources, and resistance to economic activities that threaten the landscape and its natural heritage. For PCC, this has also an economic component, preserving the natural heritage and landscape guarantees the quality of coffee and becomes an important tourist attraction.

Local development and neoliberalism

Although adapting and rejecting neoliberal policies are not part of the objectives of PCC or Coopeumo (not directly), through this type of regional cooperation process, neoliberal economic policies can be adapted and rejected at the local level, influencing local development agendas (Morales, 2021).

What is rejected and what is adapted depend on the local interpretations of neoliberalism itself (Morales, 2021). When neoliberalism is understood as the expansion of extractive activities, PCC rejects its policies by promoting conservation of natural resources and traditional modes of production. Neoliberal policies are undesirable when the natural and cultural attributes are threatened, for example, PCC became a tool to oppose mining projects despite the promises of economic growth brought up with those types of projects. At the same time, PCC promotes strategies to improve regional competitiveness, innovation, and productive agglomerations, typical elements of neoliberal economic development. Coopeumo, on the other hand, embraces neoliberalism as an economic model that promotes exports and the free market but rejects it when it is seen as a political project that ended social and community wellbeing. Coopeumo's main concern is to contribute to increasing the incomes of its members, and the strategies to do so have changed over time: While in its origins was helping farmers to gain and retain land ownership, today it focuses on improving production by providing technical assistance, reaching agreements with universities to adapt agricultural machinery to smaller fields, or finding markets inside and outside of Chile. Coopeumo does not openly oppose neoliberal economic policies when they involve exports and markets, but its work ensures that more people can benefit from that model (Morales, 2021).

Development for whom?

The answer to this question seems simpler for Coopeumo. The cooperative is concerned about its members, their families, and the rural communities where they live, and sets out to address their specific production and wellbeing needs, yet not (directly) seeking to impact the wider territory. With PCC the answer is more complex. PCC was intended to benefit and preserve the territory, that is, the combination of a natural and institutional landscape with a cultural heritage, including a series of cultural, social, and economic practices. However, by consolidating itself as a regional brand, PCC has served to oppose mining projects, but also to sell tourist services and urban developments that threaten the landscape, traditional production, and ecosystems.

The tourist industry deserves special attention. Some argue that the growth of the tourism sector is an inevitable outcome of being part of the UNESCO heritage list. This can have a positive effect as it can help diversify the local economy and create new jobs; however, there are also concerns about the consequences of mass tourism on the ecosystems and the carrying capacities in rural municipalities (where most visitors concentrate). Another area of concern is the distribution of economic benefits, as indicated by the interviewees; so far, the greatest beneficiaries are those who already owned land and held greater technical and financial capacity (mostly the local economic elites), and not those who PCC sets out to aid.

Conclusions

This chapter explained processes of regional cooperation aimed at advancing local development agendas from the point of view of two different types of cooperative arrangements: PCC and Coopeumo. Regional cooperation refers to the joint and coordinated work of a series of actors who would otherwise be independent of each other. In both cases, contexts of social inequality, poverty, and inappropriate top-down policies became the main reasons for private sector and academic actors to intervene by creating cooperative organisations, as has also been observed in other Latin American regions (Sarria, 2002).

Regional cooperation processes can take various forms depending on the local context and the needs they seek to address. Some fit within preestablished forms contained in laws and regulations, such as inter-municipal agreements, metropolitan areas, and administrative regions, others do not have a preestablished legal definition, as is the case with PCC, or that remain in the private sector with little involvement from local authorities, as in the case of Coopeumo. However, a more remarkable aspect is how regional cooperation serves to highlight what is territory. Territories are not spaces defined by administrative boundaries but a landscape and a combination of cultural and socio-economic practices (Haesbaert, 2018, 2020). From a public policy perspective, this implies that the rules that seek to regulate cooperative processes (whether through the creation of regions, metropolitan areas, and inter-municipal arrangements, among others) need to be more flexible in relation to the territorial reach and provide more tools to guarantee the participation of local actors.

Regional cooperation processes also highlight how development is redefined according to territorial agendas. In the cases analysed here, development is not only defined and measured by the number of jobs created or exports. Development also means correcting the problems created by top-down economic and social policies, placing the context, culture, and local needs at the core of the agenda. It also means opening more spaces for more actors to actively define what type of development, territory, and landscape they want.

Bibliography

Arango-Gaviria, O. (2008). Eco-Región Eje Cafetero: Una Experiencia de Desarrollo Regional en Colombia, *ACE*, III(7).

Asher, K., and Wainwright, J. (2019). After Post-Development: On Capitalism, Difference, and Representation, *Antipode*, 51(1), 25–44. https://www.doi.org/10.1111/anti.12430

Brenner, N. (2003). Metropolitan Institutional Reform and the Rescaling of State Space in Contemporary Western Europe, *European Urban and Regional Studies*, 10(4), 297–324.

Chatterton, P., and Gordon, N. (2004). *Taking Back Control: A Journey Through Argentina's Popular Uprising*. University of Leeds.

Citroni, G., Lippi, A., and Profeti, S. (2013). Remapping the State: Inter-Municipal Cooperation through Corporatisation and Public-Private Governance Structures, *Local Government Studies*, 39(2), 208–234. https://www.doi.org/10.1080/03003930.2012.707615

Egermann, M. (2009). The Saxon triangle – a polycentric metropolitan region from an actor-oriented perspective, *Urban Research and Practice*, 2(3), 269–286. https://www.doi.org/10.1080/17535060903319186

Escobar, A. (1995). *Encountering Development: The Making and Unmaking of the Third World*. Second ed. Princeton University Press.

Escobar, A. (2010). Latin America at a crossroads: Alternative modernisations, post-liberalism, or post-development? *Cultural Studies*. https://www.doi.org/10.1080/09502380903424208

Feiock, R.C. (2005). Metropolitan governance: Conflict, competition, and cooperation, *Journal of the American Planning Association*, 71(4), 463–464.

Feiock, R.C. (2006). *Competition, Cooperation and Regional Governance*. Working Paper on Interlocal Services Cooperation. Wayne State Digital Commons.

Feiock, R.C. (2007). Rational choice and regional governance, *Journal of Urban Affairs*, 29(1), 47–63. https://www.doi.org/10.1111/j.1467-9906.2007.00322.x

Food and Agriculture Organisation of the United Nations FAO. (2012a). Cooperativas Campesinas y Seguridad Alimentaria: Un Modelo Vigente. http://www.fao.org/docrep/019/i3078s/i3078s.pdf

Food and Agriculture Organisation of the United Nations FAO (2012b) *Cooperativas Campesinas y Seguridad Alimentaria: Un Modelo Vigente*. http://www.fao.org/docrep/019/i3078s/i3078s.pdf

Gaviria Ríos, M.A., 2020. Territorialidades en la ciudad-región Eje Cafetero, Colombia. *territorios*, (42), 6–29.

Gibson-Graham, J.K. (2006) Surplus possibilities: The intentional economy of Mondragón. In: J.K. Gibson-Graham (Ed.) *A Postcapitalist Politics*. University of Minnesota Press, Mineapolis, London.

Gibson-Graham, J.K. (2008). Diverse Economies: Collaboration and Community in Economic Geography, *Progress in Human Geography*, 32(5), 613–632.

Gibson-Graham, J.K. (2011) Forging post-development partnerships. Possibilities for local and regional development. In A. Pike, A. Rodríguez-Pose, and J. Tomaney (Eds.). *Handbook of Local and Regional Development*. Routledge, London

Gillette, C.P. (2005). The conditions of interlocal cooperation, *JL & Pol.*, 21, 365.

Haesbaert, R. (2018). De categoria de análise a categoria da prática: a multiplicidade do território numa perspectiva latino-americana, *Políticas públicas e territórios: onze ensaios latino-americanos*, 267–288.

Haesbaert, R. (2020). Território(s) numa perspectiva latino-americana, *Journal of Latin American Geography*, 19(1), 141–151. https://doi.org/10.1353/lag.2020.0007

Hophmayer-Tokich, S. (2008). Inter-municipal cooperation for wastewater treatment: Case studies from Israel, *Journal of Environmental Management*, 86(3), 554–565.

Hulst, R. et al. (2009). Institutional shifts in inter-municipal service delivery, *Public Organization Review*, 9(3), 263–285. https://www.doi.org/10.1007/s11115-009-0085-8

Larner, W., and Craig, D. (2005). After neoliberalism? Local partnerships and social governance in Aotearoa New Zealand, *Antipode*, 402–424. http://www.cccg.umontreal.ca/pdf/wp6.pdf

Mackinnon, D., Cumbers, A., and Chapman, K. (2002). Learning, innovation and regional development: A critical appraisal of recent debates, *Progress in Human Geography*, 26(3), 293–312. https://www.doi.org/10.1191/0309132502ph371ra

MacLeod, G. (2001). New regionalism reconsidered: Globalization and the remaking of political economic space, *International Journal of Urban and Regional Research*, 25(4), 804–829. https://www.doi.org/10.1111/1468-2427.00345

Michie, J., Blasi, J.R., and Borzaga, C. (2017). *The Oxford Handbook of Mutual Co-operative and co-owned business*. Oxford University Press.

Morales, D. (2020). Conceptualizing sub-national regional cooperation: Coffee cultural landscape of Colombia case study, *Regions and Cohesion*, 10(1), 61–87. https://www.doi.org/10.3167/reco.2020.100105

Morales, D. (2021). Negotiating Local Development within Processes of Neoliberalisation: Empirical Evidence from a Campesinos Cooperative, *Bulletin of Latin American Research*, 1–16. https://www.doi.org/10.1111/blar.13216

Morales-Arcila, D.C. (2018). Regional cooperation and local and regional development: A comparative analysis of the Coffee Region (Colombia) and O'Higgins (Chile). Doctorate Thesis. Newcastle University.

Nelles, J., and Durand, F. (2014). Political rescaling and metropolitan governance in cross-border regions: Comparing the cross-border metropolitan areas of Lille and Luxembourg, *European Urban and Regional Studies*, 21(1), 104–122. https://www.doi.org/10.1177/0969776411431103

North, D. (1998). *La teoría económica neo-institucionalista y el desarrollo latinoamericano*. Proyecto PNUD Red para la Gobernabilidad y el Desarrollo en América Latina.

Oakerson, R.J. (2007). The study of metropolitan governance. En: R. Feiock (Ed.), *Metropolitan Governance: Conflict, Competition, and Cooperation*. Georgetown University Press.

Ortega-Melo, F. (2006). *Estudio e identificación de clúster exportadores regionales región de O'Higgins*. Informe Principal. PROCHILE.

Ostry, J., Loungani, P., and Furceri, D. (2016). *Neoliberalism: Oversold? - Instead of delivering growth, some neoliberal policies have increased inequality, in turn jeopardizing durable expansion*, (May), pp. 1–6. https://www.elibrary.imf.org/view/journals/022/0053/002/article-A013-en.xml

PCC. (2009). *Paisaje Cultural Cafetero*. Plan de Manejo. Available at https://paisajeculturalcafetero.org.co/wp-content/uploads/2022/10/plandemanejopcc.pdf (last accessed 28.11.2024)

PCC. (2010). Dossier. Quinta ed. Pereira Risaralda Available at https://sueje.edu.co/wp-content/uploads/2020/06/pcc-5ta-edici%C3%B3n.pdf

Perkmann, M. (2002). The rise of the Euroregion. A bird's eye perspective on European cross-border co-operation, *Department of Sociology*, 1–19. http://www.comp.lancs.ac.uk/sociology/papers/Perkmann-Rise-of-Euroregion.pdf
Perkmann, M. (2003). Cross-Border Regions in Europe, *European Urban and Regional Studies*, 10(2), 153–171. https://www.doi.org/10.1177/0969776403010002004
Perkmann, M. (2007) Construction of new territorial scales: A framework and case study of the EUROREGION cross-border region, *Regional Studies*, 41(2), 253–266.
Perreault, T. (2006). From the Guerra del Agua to the Guerra del Gas: Resource governance, neoliberalism and popular protest in Bolivia, *Antipode*, 38(1), 150–172. https://www.doi.org/10.1111/j.0066-4812.2006.00569.x
Pike, A., Rodríguez-Pose, A., and Tomaney, J. (2007). What kind of local and regional development and for whom?, *Regional Studies*, 41(9), 1253–1269. https://www.doi.org/10.1080/00343400701543355
Pike, A., Rodríguez-Pose, A., and Tomaney, J. (2011). *Handbook of Local and Regional Development*. Routledge.
PNUD (2004) *Eje Cafetero: Un Pacto por la Región*. Informe Regional de Desarrollo Humano.
Quintero-López, R. (2006) *Asociativismo municipal en América Latina: Gobiernos locales y sociedad civil*. Firsted. Abya-Yala FLACMA-DFID GTZ, Quito.
Rehner, J., Baeza, S., and Barton, J. (2016). *En Hombros de Gigantes: Una Geografía Económica del Comercio Chile-Asia*. Instituto de Geografía Universidad Católica de Chile.
Rodríguez-Oreggia, E., and Gutiérrez, R.T. (2006). La cooperación intermunicipal en México, *Gestión y Política Pública*, 15(2).
Sarria, A.M. (2002). Economía solidaria prácticas cooperativas y desarrollo local en el sur de Brasil. *Red de Revistas Científicas de América Latina y el Caribe España y Portugal, Extraordin*, 41–59.
Spicer, Z. (2015). Cooperation, coordination and competition: Why do municipalities participate in economic development alliances? *Canadian Public Administration*, 58(4), 549–573. https://www.doi.org/10.1111/capa.12133
Toro-Zuluaga, G. (2004). Eje Cafetero Colombiano: Compleja Historia de Caficultura Violencia y Desplazamiento, *Revista de Ciencias Humanas Universidad Tecnológica de Pereira*, 35, 127–149.
Whyte, W.F. (1995). Learning from the Mondragón cooperative experience, *Studies in Comparative International Development*, 30(2), 58–67.
Ziai, A. (2007). Development Discourse and its critics. An introduction to post-development. In: A. Ziai (Ed.) *Exploring post-development. Theory and practice problems and perspectives*. Routledge.

10 Territorialisation of drug dealing in marginalised neighbourhoods of the Costa Rican capital

Sebastián Saborío

Introduction

A multiplicity of social actors can give life to different territories (Ballvé, 2012). It is a mistake to think that the territory is produced only by the political and legal processes of the state, or that the state is the only one capable of producing forms of hegemonic power (idem). In recent years, there has been increased interest in understanding territorialisation processes in which non-state organisations and actors play a leading role, especially when they compete for access and control of local resources (Rasmussen and Lund, 2018). At the local micro-scale, such as neighbourhoods, those can be illegal actors and groups involved in drug dealing and other criminal activities (Saborío, 2019a).

This chapter demonstrates that drug-dealing groups in Rincón Grande de Pavas engage in limited territorialisation processes mainly focused on ensuring that their drug sales remain unaffected. The researched area consists of a group of neighbourhoods in San José, the capital of Costa Rica. Conflicts related to drug transactions are frequent in this area (Aguilar and Acuña, 2011), directly impacting the number of homicides. According to official statistics, there were 147 intentional homicides in Pavas between 2010 and 2018, representing 22% of the total intentional homicides in the canton of San José (OIJ, 2019).

Rincón Grande is part of the Pavas district, which has notable peculiarities. Pavas is one of the most densely populated districts in Costa Rica. It ranks low on the Social Development Index, with most of its social indicators being unfavourable (Municipality of San José, 2017). The district is characterised by significant inequality and segregation. The eastern part includes high-income areas like Rohrmoser, while the northwest, including Rincón Grande, is marked by high population density, overcrowded conditions, and deficiencies in infrastructure, green spaces, and recreational areas. According to the National Population and Housing Census by the National Institute of Statistics and Censuses (INEC, 2011), there are 680 informal settlements, and many homes are in precarious conditions.

Rincón Grande has another peculiarity: the presence of multiple illegal groups involved in drug dealing. In some cases, these groups compete for control of their territories, employing methods and capabilities similar to

DOI: 10.4324/9781032650241-12

those of armed actors challenging state power in civil war contexts (Saborío, 2019b). One key insight from the literature on territoriality and civil wars is that the weaker the state, the greater the likelihood that non-state armed actors will succeed in their efforts to control territories (De la Calle and Sánchez, 2012). Thus, literature analysing these conflicts can provide valuable insights into understanding the territorialisation of drug dealing. However, the differences in scale, conflict intensity, and the objectives of those involved in drug dealing necessitate specific research to fully comprehend the nuances of this phenomenon. The main argument of this chapter is that it cannot be assumed that drug-dealing groups inherently establish forms of territorial control. To determine whether such forms of control exist, it is necessary to conduct studies that analyse the specific social contexts in which these groups operate. For instance, the case of Rincón Grande de Pavas clearly shows that drug dealers there are not able to carry out effective territorialisation processes.

The chapter is organised as follows: The second section discusses the theoretical framework, focusing on the utility of the concepts of territoriality and territorialisation for studying groups involved in retail drug sales. The third section outlines the methodology used in the research. The fourth and fifth sections present the research findings, demonstrating these groups' inability to assert control over the neighbourhoods of Rincón Grande de Pavas or impose rules of behaviour on its residents. The chapter ends with the final section, summarising the key conclusions.

Territory, territoriality, and territorialisation

The concepts of territoriality and territory allow us to analyse how different actors implement actions to control the resources of a given geographical space. Studying these processes from the perspective of non-state actors is essential for understanding local social and economic dynamics, as well as the impact these actors have on the development of these spaces. Using the concepts of territory and territoriality to analyse how crime unfolds in a specific geographical space is particularly useful for understanding the social relations established between the different actors involved in this phenomenon.

This research focuses on drug dealing and the territorialisation processes that derive from it, as it is the most prevalent criminal activity in Rincón Grande. Drug dealing, which involves the buying and selling of supplies for personal consumption (Raffo López and Gómez Calderón, 2017), occurs in specific territories and is frequently associated with the territorialisation of urban spaces. When discussing territory in this context, it refers not just to the physical space where the drug dealer operates but to a space with controlled access and established power relations (Haesbaert and Canossa, 2011). Controlling access to an area and establishing power relations are crucial both for exploiting the resources of a particular territory and for controlling the movements of people and goods (Haesbaert and Canossa, 2011). In the case of drug dealing, the space is primarily used for the sale of drugs.

The concept of territory differs from the concepts of territoriality and territorialisation. Territoriality is defined as 'the attempt to affect, influence, or control actions and interactions (of people, things, and relationships) through the delimitation and control over a geographical area' (Sack, 1983, pp. 55). In the context of drug dealing, the control and management of the territory that facilitates drug sales can be understood as the territoriality of drug dealing. In other words, the controlled geographic area becomes both the territory and a resource of the drug trade. Territorialisation is the strategy used to control the resources of a specific area, involving the creation and implementation of a resource control system capable of establishing new forms of authority (Rasmussen and Lund, 2018). In drug-dealing contexts, the neighbourhood is transformed into a 'territory of strategy' (Ordóñez Valverde, 2017, pp. 117), where confrontation between criminal groups, and between these groups and the state, creates new authorities on a local, micro scale.

Another strength of using the notion of territoriality to analyse crime is that it allows us to understand the conflicts between the actors who utilise the geographical space. To analyse how crime unfolds spatially, Villamizar and Pobre (2018) propose five dimensions of the territory (geographical, political, economic, social, and cultural) to examine the territorial reality of a marginalised neighbourhood in Medellín, Colombia. These authors conclude that the criminal groups in Comuna Ocho in Medellín territorialised themselves in the economic dimension through the exploitation of local resources for their specific economic interests and activities, such as drug dealing and extortion (Villamizar and Pobre, 2018). On the other hand, their territorialisation is more limited regarding the social and geographical dimensions, as they encounter disputes with police forces over control of physical space and social ties with the community. This dynamic is also reflected in the Costa Rican case presented in this chapter, as will be explained in the next section. Therefore, it is crucial to avoid thinking of the territorialisation of drug-dealing gangs as a unidirectional process and instead incorporate the relationships these groups generate with community inhabitants and security forces, and how these affect the criminal groups' attempts to control resources.

An example of the above can be observed in the Honduran case, where Berg and Carranza (2016, 2018) show that high levels of community organisation difficults territorial control by criminal groups. This case can be read as a dispute between two territorialisation processes, which impact each other. Following Villamizar and Pobre (2018) and Haesbaert and Canossa (2011), we can then speak of multiterritoriality as a constant dispute between the actors who impose their interests and their particular conception of the territory. As Gutiérrez Rivera (2012) would say, the gangs' strategy determines their ability to control the territory. The analysis of territoriality must consider the classification of an area, the communication of possession-exclusion of an area, and the ability to impose control and authority over a classified place, topics that will be developed in the following sections on the case study of Rincón Grande de Pavas.

According to what has been presented so far, for there to be territorial control in drug-dealing, the territory needs to be understood as a space with exploitable resources (in this case, an intangible resource, that is, the possibility of selling drugs), where territorialization processes take place (such as the ideation and implementation of a strategy capable of creating new forms of local authority with the aim of selling drugs), that create a new territoriality (the effective and practiced authority of a group that sells drugs).

Methodology

This research used a case study methodology and qualitative analysis. The main data collection techniques were semi-structured interviews, which offer flexibility for the interviewer to adjust the question guide while carrying out the interview, so that the questions are understandable to the person interviewed (Díaz-Bravo et al., 2013, pp. 163). The objective of the interviews was to understand the 'field of forces' (Haesbaert and Canossa, 2011, pp. 69) involved in the drug-dealing groups in Rincón Grande de Pavas and the social relationships that it generates.

A total of 67 interviews were conducted, recorded, and transcribed, in addition to about three hours of unrecorded interviews. Most participants are residents of Rincón Grande de Pavas, many of them community leaders. Specifically, two interviews were conducted for the community of La Franja; three for the communities of Lomas del Río I, Lomas del Río II, and Los Laureles; four for the communities of Metrópolis II, Metrópolis III, Oscar Felipe, and Bribrí; and five interviews for Finca San Juan and Metrópolis I, respectively. Other interviews were conducted with incarcerated individuals who are serving prison sentences for their links to criminal gangs. Interviews were also held with representatives of the Judicial Investigation Agency (OIJ), the Penitentiary Police, and the Police of the Municipality of San José, with political leaders and heads of religious centres, owners of small local businesses, and employees of public institutions who carry out their work in the area under study. To proceed with the interviews, the researcher made a total of 43 visits to Rincón Grande de Pavas, 5 visits to penitentiary centres (UAI Reinaldo Villalobos and the Jorge Arturo Montero Castro Comprehensive Care Centre) and to the Ministry of Security, the offices of the OIJ, the San José Municipal Police, the Penitentiary Police, and the Municipality of San José.

Conducting interviews about drug sales in contexts where this activity involves violence and intimidation is challenging. People living in such vulnerable situations are often wary of the interviewer's intentions. Consequently, to safeguard their safety, they may refuse to participate in the interview, or if they do agree, they might not speak openly and could withhold relevant information. Aware of these difficulties, the researcher implemented a fieldwork strategy that prioritised ethical considerations (Galán Pérez, 2011). This involved finding suitable interview locations that ensured the privacy of the interviewees, allowing them to feel comfortable knowing that no one else could hear them. Additionally, the researcher explained the intended use of the data, assured the interviewees that their names would not appear in any publication, and sought their permission to record the interview. The interviewees were informed that they could stop the recording at any time to ask questions, say something off the record, avoid discussing certain topics, or stop the interview completely. This strategy fostered an environment where interviewees felt more open and confident about participating.

Primary data collection also included mapping activities conducted at the end of each interview with residents of the Rincón Grande de Pavas communities. The goal of this activity was to generate heat maps or hot spot maps, which presented drug sales as individual points or clusters when sales covered larger areas along public roads. Darker colours on the map indicate a greater number of residents agreeing on the location of specific drug sale points (see Figure 10.1). These maps enabled the geographical analysis of crime, as crimes are not distributed uniformly across space (Eck et al., 2005). The maps helped locate drug sale points and spatially identify the drug-dealing gangs operating locally. Mapping with residents allowed them to pinpoint locations and areas where they had identified drug sales. This approach leveraged the residents' knowledge and experiences, as they are the individuals who deal daily with the implications of the presence of drug gangs in their area.

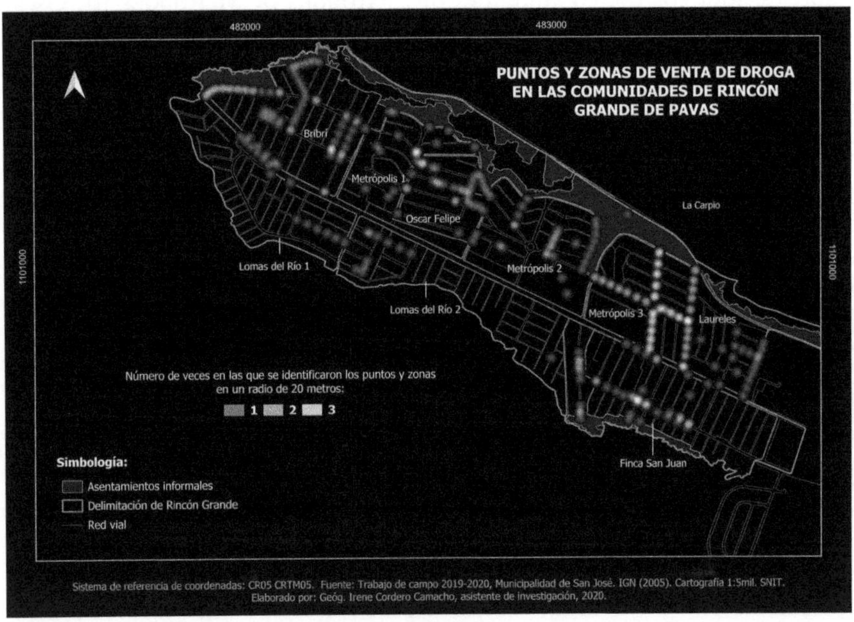

Figure 10.1 Heat map of drug sales identified by residents. Author.

'No, we don't have that mapped': Territoriality, classification of an area, and the communication of possession-exclusion

Territoriality comprises three key elements: the classification of an area, the communication of possession or exclusion, and the ability to impose control and authority over a designated space. Classification refers to the ability of a group or person to establish possession over a specific area (Gutiérrez Rivera, 2012). In the context of drug dealing, although this activity predominantly occurs in public spaces, such usage alone does not necessarily establish long-term possession of the area. Possession is directly signalled by the consistent and stable presence of individuals from a gang engaged in drug sales at a particular location. For example, when gang members sell drugs regularly from a corner of a neighbourhood, a street, or a park, they effectively establish control over that area. This control persists until another group—whether another gang, the police, or a community organisation—successfully takes over the area, either by eliminating the initial group or by forcing them to relocate.

In Rincón Grande de Pavas, most drug sales occur in public spaces, particularly on street sidewalks and in certain recreational areas. Residents have reported that drug sales and associated violence have led them to restrict sports and other recreational activities in these areas due to safety concerns. Figure 10.1 illustrates the locations where residents have identified drug sales. Notably, five of the six largest parks and squares in Rincón Grande de Pavas are among the sites used by criminal groups for drug transactions. This aligns with Groff and McCord's (2012) observation that public spaces, such as parks, often become contested areas. Due to their public nature and the absence of formal or informal management authority, these spaces can attract illicit activities, creating a conflict of interest between legitimate users and those who exploit these areas for criminal purposes.

The map reveals that drug sale points are predominantly concentrated in the northern communities of Rincón Grande, specifically in Los Laureles, Metrópolis III, Metrópolis II, Oscar Felipe, Metrópolis I, and Bribrí. These areas account for 58 of the 75 drug sale points identified in the cartography conducted with local residents. Both the residents of Rincón Grande and members of the Public Force agree that drug sales primarily occur in three types of spaces: public streets, bunkers, and some residential houses. On public streets, drug sales are typically concentrated at street corners, where two gang members are usually stationed. Their roles include selling drugs and monitoring for police presence, with one member, known as the 'bell', who is responsible for alerting the others to any approaching law enforcement. Bunkers, the second type of space, are structures such as abandoned houses or businesses used for drug storage and sales (Hernández Ulloa, 2018). These bunkers are not only sites for drug transactions but also places where individuals may stay to consume drugs. The third type of space is residential houses where drug sales occur. These houses are managed by their occupants, who conduct quick transactions to minimise suspicion. According to the police, these residences generally do not store large quantities of drugs due to the risk of break-ins, which limits their ability to hide the merchandise.

Residents report that armed conflicts often erupt near drug sale points, posing risks to people engaged in everyday activities such as work, study, and recreation. The study's findings indicate that no single group currently monopolises drug distribution across a large area in Rincón Grande de Pavas. Instead, multiple groups operate in the area, with varying degrees of clarity about their identities and territories. For instance, when asked about the number of drug-selling groups in her neighbourhood, one participant replied, 'No, we don't have that mapped' (interview 53, recorded, woman, 2/18/2020), while another said, 'I can't tell you if the guy from gang 'x' is selling drugs here and the guy from gang 'y' is selling drugs there. I don't know, no' (interview 30, recorded, man, 7/17/2019).

The Judicial Investigation Organization (OIJ) identifies three gangs in Rincón Grande de Pavas, whereas the Public Force reports at least eight groups. Residents and individuals who have been incarcerated suggest that the actual number may be even higher. For example, one inmate, who belonged to a gang before his arrest, claims that every street in Lomas (a part of Rincón Grande) hosts a small criminal group. Other interviewees mention up to five gangs in Bribrí alone, though some estimate only three. Residents of Lomas II and Oscar Felipe report three gangs each, while numbers vary for Los Laureles, Metropolis I, and Finca San Juan. The frequent changes in the 'ownership' of sale points due to gang disputes and occasional co-presence of multiple gangs in the same area reflect a limited capacity for territorial control. This fragmentation suggests that a more dominant group, if it existed, would likely prevent the presence of other gangs in the same space.

The multiplicity and diffuse nature of the spaces classified for the exercise of drug sale activities highlights the importance of evaluating the way in which drug-dealing groups exercise the second element of territoriality, that is, the communication of possession-exclusion of an area. This element involves the communication or signalling of possession of the delimited area (Gutiérrez Rivera, 2012, pp. 170) and can be carried out, for example, by placing visible symbols or signs, so that people outside a group know that they possess the marked space (Sack, 1983), as can be seen in Figure 10.2. The photo shows how Los Diablos gang employs murals to assert control over specific areas of Rincón Grande de Pavas. However, this tactic is not universally adopted by all criminal groups. Many gangs do not have clearly visible or exclusive control over their drug sale points, and their dominance is often not recognised or acknowledged by residents in the area.

Among the numerous criminal groups operating in Rincón Grande de Pavas, few manage to establish clear and respected boundaries, both within the community and among rival gangs. The establishment and defence of such borders signify power, demonstrating that those who create them possess the strength to enforce their rules and protect their territory from

Figure 10.2 Mural showcasing a gang symbol on a wall in Rincón Grande de Pavas. Photograph taken during fieldwork in May 2019. Author.

external encroachments (Chávez Verduzco, 2015). In contrast, the absence of identifiable borders indicates a lack of territorial control and resource extraction capability (Rasmussen and Lund, 2018). For gangs, the key resource is the space in which they sell drugs. The lack of clear borders suggests that these groups either lack the power to engage in territorial conflicts or, when such conflicts occur, they do not lead to decisive control by any one group.

The third element of territoriality—the ability to impose control and authority over a designated area—will be examined in the following section.

'Each to his own and we all live in peace': The ability to impose spatial control and authority

The territorialisation processes observed in Rincón Grande de Pavas are reflected in the ability of drug-dealing gangs to impose control and authority over specific areas. This control is exercised by determining who can enter a given space and influencing the actions and interactions of people within it (Gutiérrez Rivera, 2012). Unlike state organisations, such as police forces, which operate under regulated legal frameworks and hold coercive power, criminal gang leaders acquire power through the use of unregulated violence (Koivu, 2016). For drug-dealing groups, this violence facilitates their rise to power and enables them to establish authority. The territorialisation by these gangs allows them to create and enforce informal legal systems. However, the scope of their territorial control depends on whether they can integrate only their own members or extend their influence to include other residents. Understanding the extent of their control involves examining both the number of people and the spatial reach of their authority. A group dedicated to drug dealing, which typically obtains its position of power through the use and threat of use of force, can carry out territorialisation processes and establish authority capable of ruling and implementing rules that make up informal legal systems. Said territorialisation, however, may have more or less scope, depending on whether it is able to integrate under its control only the members of the same gang or whether its power also manages to include other people. If it does, it becomes necessary to know how many people and the spatial extent this authority covers.

Territorialisation involves not only the establishment of authority but also the creation of a system of rules that residents must understand and follow (Rasmussen and Lund, 2018). Effective territorialisation requires monitoring the enforcement of these rules and applying punishments to those who violate them. In Rincón Grande de Pavas, drug gangs actively monitor various locations, particularly corners and other drug sale points, as well as entrances to residential areas and main streets. They employ members on foot, on motorcycles, or in cars to detect whether unknown individuals or vehicles belong to rival gangs or are police officers. Interviews revealed that gang leaders assign subordinates to surveillance roles and equip them with weapons. Some residents of Oscar Felipe and Villa Esperanza (a community southeast of Rincón Grande) expressed frustration over the installation of surveillance cameras by gangs in public spaces. Besides physical patrols and cameras, gangs also use radios similar to those of the police and apps like WhatsApp to receive updates from 'pirate' (informal) taxi drivers.

Despite this extensive surveillance, residents are not typically stopped or interrogated by gangs. Criminal groups primarily focus on detecting the presence of rival gang members and police to prevent territorial incursions and avoid detection. Police forces in Rincón Grande de Pavas can enter any area at any time, often patrolling in vehicles but also on foot. The presence of police leads drug dealers to hide or flee, and confrontations with law enforcement are usually aimed at avoiding arrests rather than preventing police access to neighbourhoods.

To assess whether criminal groups can impose authority on residents in the analysed area, it was crucial to determine if these groups had established conduct standards. The findings confirmed that they do, prompting an investigation into the nature of these norms and the groups' ability to enforce them through potential punishments. Interviewees reported that criminal groups have set a code of conduct affecting specific aspects of daily life. One interviewee described it as follows:

> Well, as long as you know the rules of the game, it is very important, each one does his own thing and we all live in peace, I know that (…). Normally the rules are: you don't know anything, you don't see anything, if you saw, you didn't see and if you know, you don't know (…) For example, if you see someone selling, a conflict that you go and collaborate, seeing, saying, where to find someone because they are looking for you. One knows nothing, one sees nothing, each to his own. Everyone respects the rules and that's it.
>
> (Interview 18, recorded, woman, 5/29/2019)

Residents avoid alerting authorities about criminal activities to prevent retaliation against themselves or their families. Interfering with gang operations can lead to threats, eviction, or even murder. Generally, gangs focus on drug sales and do not seek to monopolise violence or intervene in domestic disputes, unlike in some other Latin American countries (Rodgers and Baird, 2016). Gangs tend to get involved in cases of interpersonal violence only if it involves their family members or close associates. Although there were mentions of gangs intervening in domestic violence and sexual abuse in the past, such involvement appears to be rare now. In some instances, gangs also limit or prevent robberies on public roads to avoid attracting police attention to their drug sales points. Opinions on whether gangs still prohibit such crimes vary. In Finca San Juan, Metrópolis I, Metrópolis II, and informal settlements bordering Los Laureles, some residents believe gangs still enforce prohibitions, punishing members who break these rules with violence.

Creating full authority within a territory involves displacing existing power structures and establishing new territorialities. In the studied context, while state presence is noted, it is often limited to police control and repression rather than broader social welfare. The research indicates that drug-dealing gangs do not seek to monopolise power or overthrow the state, unlike insurrectional groups. Instead, their authority coexists with state power, civil associations, and other local forces (Doyle, 2016). When gangs have significant control, they can influence local political power and daily life management, roles typically filled by community organisations and political parties under legal conditions (Wolff, 2015). The infiltration of criminal groups in political activity occurs, at the community level, especially when they manage to achieve a criminal monopoly in a certain territory, which gives them the tranquillity and strength necessary to expand their room for manoeuvre (Magaloni et al., 2020). For this reason, it is not surprising that in Rincón Grande de Pavas gangs do not play a role in local associations. Indeed, the number of drug-dealing groups and conflicts over control over points of sale do not allow them to focus on this type of activity.

Most of the community leaders in Rincón Grande mentioned that they try to have a good relationship with the members of the drug gangs. This does not mean that close ties are generated but rather that they try to have cordial relations that allow the peaceful coexistence of both parties. This includes, for example, people greeting each other when they meet on the street, or solving problems through dialogue. Some of the leaders, mainly the older ones, consider that the criminal groups respect them because they have a certain authority at the community level and because they have known them for a long time, some of them even since they were children.

Those interviewed stated that there have been no homicides or physical attacks against community leaders, but there have been threats against them. Two community leaders commented that years ago they were threatened by local drug gangs. The first case occurred when a community leader opposed the gang's intentions to acquire land to expand their sales. In the second case, the threats came when another leader challenged the presence of some young members of the gangs who were causing damage to their community. Once again, we see that friction and conflicts between residents and drug dealers only occur when the former put obstacles in the way of the latter's activity. Apart from these two cases, which occurred in the past, the results of the investigation indicate that, in general, community leaders (and even their relatives) are respected by criminal groups, which have not shown any interest in influencing the activity of community organisations or their decision-making processes. Likewise, in an interview it was mentioned that the people who collaborate in the worship centres of Rincón Grande de Pavas are also respected by the members of the gangs.

As can be observed, the actions and strategies that drug-dealing groups exercise over the territory are limited and do not manage to generate new forms of local authority or dominance. In other words, territorialisation processes are limited to facilitating and maintaining drug sales. These are manifested through strategies such as the imposition of the 'law of silence', the control of robberies, and the surveillance of drug sales areas but, unlike what happens in other Latin American contexts, in Rincón Grande de Pavas, territorialisation processes do not manage other aspects of the daily life of the communities in which they are positioned.

Conclusions

The empirical contribution of this chapter is to demonstrate that the drug gangs in Rincón Grande de Pavas employ weak territorialisation strategies. These gangs do not aim to achieve comprehensive territorial control beyond the drug trade, resulting in very limited territoriality. No single criminal group has a monopoly on the illicit drug trade in the area. Furthermore, gangs often fail to exclusively control drug sale points, particularly those in public spaces, which are frequently contested. The high number of drug-dealing groups, fragmented drug-sale locations, and residents' uncertainty about the number and identities of these gangs highlight the limited ability of these groups to consistently dominate their areas of operation. In summary, territories in Rincón Grande de Pavas are characterised by weak and fragmented control by drug gangs, with a focus on specific drug sale points rather than comprehensive territorial dominance. This dynamic reflects a broader struggle for control and highlights the challenges of managing and intervening in areas with significant criminal activity.

Regarding their relationship with the local residents, drug gangs establish authority primarily through rules and codes of conduct that allow drug sales. Their main prohibitions are to avoid reporting drug activities to the police, not to obstruct drug sales, and to ensure debts for consumed drugs are paid. The gangs' surveillance focuses mainly on monitoring rival gang members and police forces, without attempting to restrict their access or influence residents' behaviour beyond these areas. However, the competition for control over public spaces, such as street corners and parks, highlights the dynamic and contested nature of territory in this context. Public spaces are frequently disputed, and drug sale points often change hands among different gangs. This constant conflict over these spaces reflects a broader struggle for dominance and control within the neighbourhood.

The situation in Rincón Grande de Pavas provides an illustration of how territory functions as a social construct influenced by a combination of cultural, economic, social, and spatial factors, including illegal activities. In this context, drug gangs exert control over the territory through informal rules and codes of conduct that dictate certain social interactions. The social structures within Rincón Grande de Pavas also play a crucial role in territorial formation. The gangs' ability to enforce their own systems of power and authority reflects a social order where traditional forms of authority, such as law enforcement, are less effective. This situation results in a unique form of territorial control that is recognised and adhered to by residents, primarily due to the threat of violence and retaliation.

Spatially, the organisation of territory is evident in the contestation of public spaces such as street corners and parks, which are frequently targeted by criminal groups. These public spaces, being more accessible and less regulated, become focal points for territorial disputes and control. The use of surveillance and monitoring by gangs to oversee these areas exemplifies how the physical environment is intertwined with social mechanisms of control. Further, this reinforces the notion that territory is constructed not only through the presence of institutional forces but also through their absence, even if in this case this absence is reflected in criminal and illegal activities.

Understanding the nature and extent of gang control is crucial for effective public policy. The presence of multiple, fragmented criminal groups and their limited territorial authority can impact the implementation and success of social programmes and interventions. Policies need to be tailored to address the specific realities of gang control and territorial dynamics to be effective in such contexts. Indeed, this research suggests that to devise and implement public policies in contexts characterised by the presence of criminal groups dedicated to the sale of drugs, it is crucial to understand in advance whether said groups control the territory in which they are located. This is because the control exercised by criminal groups can hinder the actions that social programmes or other forms of public policy attempt to carry out and, in this way, limit or nullify the expected results. In this way, national and local authorities reduce the possibility of proposing ineffective solutions to solve or reduce social problems in contexts characterised by high levels of social exclusion. Furthermore, it is not enough to understand whether these groups control the territory, because if they do, it is needed to identify the type of control they have. This because each type of control is exercised through different strategies according to the reality of the local context.

Bibliography

Aguilar, O.G.R., and Acuña, A.S.S. (2011). Pandillas, violencia y dinámicas socioculturales en la Costa Rica urbana, *Intersticios Sociales*, (1), 1–42.

Ballvé, T. (2012). Everyday state formation: territory, decentralization, and the narco landgrab in Colombia, *Environment and Planning D: Society and Space*, 30(4), 603–622.

Berg, L. and Carranza, I. (2016). *Propuesta de vivienda de "interés social" para el precario "El Relleno, Finca San Juan de Rincón Grande" en Pavas. [Proyecto de Graduación]*. Escuela de Arquitectura y Urbanismo, Instituto Tecnológico de Costa Rica.

Berg, L., and Carranza, M. (2018). Organized criminal violence and territorial control, *Journal of Peace Research*, 55(5), 566–581. doi: 10.1177/0022343317752796

Chávez, B.V. (2015). *Cada quien su imperio: Preferencias institucionales y patrones territoriales de inseguridad*. Editorial Universitaria|Libros UDG.

De la Calle, L., and Sánchez-Cuenca, I. (2012). Rebels without a territory: An analysis of nonterritorial conflicts in the world, 1970–1997, *Journal of Conflict Resolution*, 56(4), 580–603.

Díaz-Bravo, L., Torruco-García, U., Martínez-Hernández, M., and Varela-Ruiz, M. (2013). La entrevista, recurso flexible y dinámico, *Investigación en educación médica*, 2(7), 162–167.

Doyle, C. (2016). Explaining patterns of urban violence in Medellin, Colombia. *Laws*, 5(1), 3.

Eck, J., et al. (2005). *Mapping crime: Understanding Hot Spots*. National Institute of Justice.

Galán, B.P. (2011). "Y esto, a mí, ¿para qué me sirve, señorita?". Implicaciones éticas y políticas de la etnografía en contextos de violencia, pobreza y desigualdad. Ankulegi, *Revista de Antropología Social*, (15), 103–114.

Groff, E., and McCord, E.S. (2012). The role of neighborhood parks as crime generators, *Security journal*, 25(1), 1–24.

Haesbaert, R., and Canossa, M. (2011). *El mito de la desterritorialización: del "fin de los territories" a la multiterritorialidad*. México: Siglo XXI.

Hernández Ulloa, F. (2018). Consumismo en Costa Rica: una tipología de jóvenes en contextos urbanos de exclusión social, *Anuario de Estudios Centroamericanos*, 44, 429–462.

INEC. (2011). *Población total proyectada al 30 de junio por grupos de edades, según provincia, cantón, distrito y sexo. Proyecciones Nacionales*. Estadísticas demográficas 2011–2025, Instituto Nacional de Estadística y Censos.

Koivu, K.L. (2016). In the shadow of the state: mafias and illicit markets, *Comparative Political Studies*, 49(2), 155–183.

Magaloni, B., Franco-Vivanco, E., and Melo, V. (2020). Killing in the slums: Social order, criminal governance, and police violence in Rio de Janeiro, *American Political Science Review*, 114(2), 552–572.

Municipalidad de San José. (2017). *Plan de Desarrollo Municipal 2017–2020, Plan de mediano plazo*. Dirección de Planificación Estratégica Institucional, Municipalidad de San José.

Ordóñez Valverde, J. (2017). De la pandilla a la banda. Transformaciones de la violencia pandillera en barrios marginales en Cali, *Sociedad y economía*, (32), 107–126.

Organismo de Investigación Judicial (OIJ). 2019. *Comunicación personal. Solicitud de información 571-OPO/UAC/S-2019*. Homicidios dolosos en Pavas.

Raffo López, L., and Gómez Calderón, D. 2017. Redes criminales y corrupción en la era del microtráfico y el narcomenudeo. *Revista de Economía Institucional* 19, 227–261. https://doi.org/10.18601/01245996.v19n37.12

Rasmussen, M.B., and Lund, C. (2018). Reconfiguring Frontier Spaces: The territorialization of resource control, *World Development*, 101, 388–399.
Rivera, L.G. (2012). Geografías de violencia y exclusión: pandillas encarceladas en Honduras, *Latin American Research Review*, 167–179.
Rodgers, D., and Baird, A. (2016). Entender a las pandillas de América Latina: una revisión de la literatura, *Revista Estudios Socio-Jurídicos*, 18(1), 13–53.
Saborío, S. (2019a). Narcomenudeo y control territorial en América Latina, *URVIO Revista Latinoamericana de Estudios de Seguridad*, (25), 71–86.
Saborío, S. 2019b. Estado del arte sobre narcoviolencia en Costa Rica State of the art on narcoviolence in Costa Rica. Reflexiones.Volumen 98 (2): 23–38.
Sack, R.D. (1983). Human territoriality: a theory, *Annals of the association of American geographers*, 73(1), 55–74.
Villamizar, A., and Pobre, W. (2018). Multiterritorialidad en la comuna 8 de Medellín a partir de la relación entre comunidad, Policía Nacional y crimen organizado, *Ciudad Paz-ando*, 11(2), 84–96. doi: https://doi.org/10.14483/2422278X.12199
Wolff, M.J. (2015). Policing and the logics of violence: a comparative analysis of public security reform in Brazil, *Policing and society*, 27(5), 560–574.

11 Conclusions

Territories and development in Latin America

Tiago Teixeira, Laura Sariego-Kluge and Diana Morales

Throughout the book, we examined the different ways in which territory and development have been conceptualised and operationalised as development policies in Latin America. Initially, modernisation theory and dependency theory were substantially discussed in Latin American academia and influential in the design and implementation of policies as top-down and universalised approaches to development. Modernisation theory framed development as a linear progression from "traditional" to "modern" societies, advocating for a shift from traditional to modern economic relations and cultural traits (Willis, 2011; Peet and Hartwick, 2009). In response, dependency theory, initially developed by Global South scholars such as Raúl Prebisch and Andre Gunder Frank, critiqued modernisation's Eurocentric assumptions. It posited that underdevelopment in Latin America stemmed from an unequal exchange, where core nations extracted resources and wealth from peripheral regions. Dependency theorists, therefore, understood that development was mainly possible by replacing imports with domestic production through the import-substitution industrialisation (ISI) model (Peet and Hartwick, 2009). Fast forward to the years of neoliberalisation, neoliberalism has guided the design of policies and initiatives around the deregulation of international trade, free capital mobility, and the privatisation of goods (Williamson, 1990; Stiglitz, 2002). The adoption of neoliberalism, nonetheless, has led to harmful and contradictory effects in Latin America from the dispossession of peasants, and suppression of rights to the commons, to the depletion of natural resources (Harvey, 2005; Perreault and Martin, 2005). Partly as a response to the historical inequalities exacerbated by neoliberal approaches, the first two decades of the 21st century saw the rise of left-leaning governments in several countries, looking to redefine development paradigms by focusing on social inclusion, poverty reduction, and wealth redistribution. This new approach to development was accompanied by nationwide constitutional changes recognising multiethnicity, rights of indigenous and Afro-Latinos communities, rights of nature, and diverse epistemologies. However, this approach also relies on the exploitation of natural resources, supported by state control over minerals, oil, and gas, doing little to alter the role of Latin American economies as providers of raw materials for global markets while

DOI: 10.4324/9781032650241-13

disregarding environmental and cultural concerns, raising several critiques amongst activists and academics (Svampa, 2015, 2019). In general, previous approaches to development have treated territories as economic assets that could be tamed to serve broader economic agendas, overlooking scale, place, and power.

The limitations of these dominating approaches to development, plus the contradictory effects of neoliberalism, prompted debates on alternative visions to territory and development, fostering some substantial theoretical advancements. These theoretical advancements have produced a body of scholarship that we identified as having a particular Latin American identity. For example, while Anglo-Saxon approaches tend to focus on territory as a space of capitalist production and economic development in the face of the intensification of globalisation, in Latin America we see a more radical approach that considers the plurality of the territory and its multiplicity of local actors and interests, including existing dynamics of power relations around exploitation and resistance (Haesbaert, 2018). Territories are not only understood under a Weberian sense (state power, administrative boundaries, and sovereign monopoly of violence) but also as a reflection of power relations (appropriation, domination, and control of territories) among various actors and institutions at different scales and dimensions (cultural, economic, political, and environmental) in a given historical moment (Saquet, 2007; Fuini, 2014; Haesbaert, 2018).

By bringing this notion of territory into development studies, Latin American scholars have proposed a decolonial approach to development, termed territorial development, which has contributed to academic development studies and discourses as well as to policy design. Such a decolonial approach to territorial development proposes development practices that take into consideration local contexts, experiences, knowledge, and interactions (within the dimensions previously mentioned and at multiple scales), including existing power struggles, conflicts, and resistances that can result in a reordering of power relations for better living conditions (Saquet, 2007, 2018; Schneider 2010). Therefore, a territorial approach to development inverts top-down development decision-making by empowering marginalised communities in light of historical injustices, and by proposing an alternative mode of development based on bottom-up conflicts, resistance, and decisions that promote sustainable practices and initiatives (Saquet, 2018).

As explained in Part 1, Latin American scholarship on territorial development has crystallized around three key analytical streams: territories as practice, the normative vision of territory, and territory as an analytical concept (Haesbaert, 2018; Lopez et al., 2017). These streams of literature can, however, intersect one another as scholars often bring these different elements together when exploring their empirical case studies. Under the stream 'territories as practice', scholars have been interested in exploring the diverse views and interpretations of territory from traditional indigenous perspectives to contrasting views based on economic and political rationalities. Such studies often explore how territorial dynamics, which are based on power relations, can change due to global and national forces (mostly focused on the impact of neoliberalism) that challenge territories' traditional worldviews and ways of life, resulting in struggles and resistance (Motoki, 2018; Haesbaert, 2018). The stream of literature termed 'normative vision of territory' is composed of studies that engage with varying notions of territory in order to propose public policies of development. While some scholars here are interested in studying how policymakers can support endogenous assets and foster competitive advantage and economic growth, others are concerned with more decolonial approaches or ways to empower local communities and break with social injustices, fostering an alternative mode of development (Maldonado-Torres, 2018; Haesbaert, 2018; Saquet and Chicoski, 2022). Finally, 'territory as an analytical concept' has also been of interest to several scholars. Under this stream of literature, scholars have proposed concepts of territory and analytical frameworks to examine territories and development. Decolonial thought is also central in such a stream of literature. Power has gained a central position in such studies as an analytical element as well as key concepts such as place, scale, territoriality, territorialisation, deterritorialisation, and reterritorialisation.

The empirical chapters of this book provide a good example of such streams of literature (or combination of) and their approaches to territory and development. For example, Chapters 5, 6, and 7 examine the contradictory impact of neoliberalism or global capitalism on territories in Argentina and Brazil, and the clash of different development worldviews. These chapters illustrate well the notion of territories as practices and the normative vision of territory. Chapter 5, for instance, examines how the advance of financial capital in Argentina has transformed peasants' territories into profit-extraction platforms, expelling traditional communities, and fostering environmental degradation—framed as a dereterritorialisation process. The authors propose an alternative form of development, with an anti-capitalism subjectivity, based on agroecology as a strategy of resistance that prioritises the reproduction of life and nature over capital accumulation, builds food and technology sovereignty, relies on ancestral knowledge, and empowers small farmers. Similarly, Chapter 5 explores the influence of technoscience on yerba mate cultivation and territorial development in the Vale do Iguaçu (Brazil). According to the authors, technoscientific approaches led by neoliberalism in Latin America often perpetuate capitalist dynamics, prioritising productivity and market integration at the expense of social, cultural, and environmental considerations. It highlights the need for development models that include local actors such as small farmers in decision-making and respect traditional practices to achieve sustainable and inclusive development. Chapter 7 investigates how neoliberal top-down infrastructure development projects in Chaco (Argentina) overlooked the general needs of local communities and resulted in land grabbing, exclusion, and dispossession. The observation of the incompatibility between a neoliberal normative perspective of territory can also be seen in Chapter 9. Through the study of Paisaje Cultural Cafetero in Colombia and the cooperative Coopeumo in Chile, the author concludes that processes of regional cooperation reflect the social and cultural aspects with which territories are perceived by their inhabitants, and not the normative territory predefined by national states. The chapter also shows that administrative boundaries can even limit the scope of cooperation processes. Such chapters exemplify how top-down models of development in Latin America, based on neoliberalism, impact territories in detrimental ways, fostering processes of deterritorialisation and power struggles over the control of the territory. Additionally, these chapters urge the need for alternative forms of development that take into consideration local communities, their knowledge, and needs.

Other chapters have explored in more detail processes of territorialisation and power relations within territories, which can also be placed under the literature of territories as practices. Chapter 10, for example, employs the concept of territoriality and territorialisation to examine the influence and level of control of drug dealing groups over Rincón Grande de Pavas in San José, Costa Rica. The author reveals that illegal activities such as drug trafficking can have profound implications on how a space is inhabited both directly by groups that commit crimes and indirectly through the actions that governments may take to try to subdue them. Chapter 10 demonstrates that territories are composed of different social groups that struggle for domination and control under legal and illegal circumstances that have a broad development impact on local communities.

Chapter 8 provides a strong example of Latin American scholarship on the relationship between territories and different forms of resistance, solidarity, and alternative development models in the face of the exclusive contradictions generated by capital. This is not only through empirical studies describing cases of 'success' but also through studies proposing ontological and epistemological changes within a decolonial perspective on how one should understand and approach territory, echoing the statements made in Chapter 4. These chapters, therefore, intersect streams of literature under the normative vision of territory and territory as an analytical concept. Chapter 8 builds upon the concept of biocultural territory to explain territories as spaces of resistance whose historical role has been to guarantee the subsistence of families like the Mayas inhabiting the Yucatan Peninsula. Here, the territory, in addition to harbouring social, cultural, and economic relations, constitutes a symbolic but dynamic space that allows the exercise of traditional ways of inhabiting the space, relating to nature, and preserving culture. In addition to being a symbolic space, the territory is also a space of resistance against dispossession. The processes of deterritorialisation and dispossession of Mayan families that in colonial times were exercised through violence, today, continue through neoliberal policies and development strategies that homogenise and commodify the territory. Nevertheless, the *Solar* remains a fundamental space that provides Mayan families with elements that facilitate their subsistence. One important contribution of this chapter is that domestic spaces, often neglected in territorial studies, are also understood as part of the territory, a scale that, while intimate, is influenced by historical and contemporary experiences with nature and culture. The *Solar* is a smaller scale, a place of habitation and a family space, and at the same time, a space of manifestation of the autonomy and exercise of the rights of Maya families. Therefore, Chapter 8 invites reflection on the scale of the territory and brings attention to alternative forms of development that respect traditional knowledge and indigenous communities. Chapter 4 questions hegemonic top-down development approaches and advocates for decolonial and counter-hegemonic practices that give centrality to social participation and grassroots knowledge, place awareness, solidarity, and local empowerment as an alternative model of territorial development. The authors propose a methodology based on several years of conducting research at the Universidade Estadual do Oeste do Paraná in Brazil, where they have established participatory action research projects with local residents to implement a grassroots, decolonial, and counter-hegemonic territorial development research method.

This book brings forth, therefore, theoretical and empirical contributions to wider debates on development studies. First, it provides a critical reflection on top-down approaches to development that often prioritise economic rationality over local needs, and, consequently, overlook the particularities of territories including their knowledge, histories, culture, and struggles. As we have discussed, such approaches suffer from territorial blindness. By emphasising on the multidimensional, multiscale nature of territories along with the multitude of actors with differential power relations, the territorial studies here presented enrich academic discourse on the complexity of development. Second, the decolonial approaches presented in this book to territory and territorial development challenge linear, evolutionary, and hegemonic perspectives to development, and contribute to existing debates by acknowledging the relevance of marginalised communities, including their worldviews, values, identities, struggles, and resistance, and by advocating for the incorporation of local voices, knowledge, solidarity, and practices in the construction of territorial development. Third, such studies can potentially contribute to the design of development policies in the public sphere. For example, many case studies presented in this book illustrated the contradictory impact of neoliberal policies for 'development' in specific territories, especially in relation to their exclusionary and detrimental effects. Such studies invite policymakers to reflect on the relevance of citizen participation and empowerment in territorial development policies for social cohesion, inclusion, and sustainable practices and initiatives. Additionally, such studies offer insights for policymakers on the relevance of understanding local communities (and their diverse range of actors and interests), their knowledge, culture, and daily lives when designing development initiatives for meaningful outcomes.

To conclude, the emergence of Latin American studies on territory and territorial development has resulted in refined understandings of the complex and multifaceted nature of development in the region. This book has explored not only how such studies have evolved theoretically but also provided several empirical cases that illustrate Latin American approaches to territory and territorial development. While these studies have contributed to academic and policymaking discourses, they are relatively recent. Consequently, there are many areas for potential development and future research. For example, there is a need for greater theoretical and empirical foundation, and more methodological rigour and clarity (Dallabrida et al., 2021). Methodologically speaking, for example, studies proposing and incorporating participatory action research are still scarce (Saquet, 2018). Moreover, while, under decolonial approaches, scholars have pointed out the importance of traditional knowledge to development, there is substantial scope to further examine how traditional knowledge can in practice inform sustainable development practices. This also encompasses examining how cultural heritages and social practices influence processes and outcomes of development. Finally, another potential area of development is related to policy-oriented research. For example, there is a need for research exploring how different forms of local governance integrate community participation in decision-making and impact development initiatives and outcomes.

Bibliography

Dallabrida, V.R., Rotta, E., Büttenbender, P.L., Denardin, V.F., and Arenhart, L.O. (2021). Abordagem territorial do desenvolvimento: categorias conceituais e pressupostos metodológicos, *Guaju*, 7(1), 8–80.

Fuini, L.L. (2014). Território e geografia no Brasil: uma revisão bibliográfica, *Formação* (Online), 1(21), 3–20.

Haesbaert, R. (2018). De categoria de análise a categoria da prática: a multiplicidade do territorio numa perspectiva latino-americana. In: F. Fridman, L. A. Gennari, & S. Lencioni (Eds.), *Políticas públicas e territorios: onze estudos latino-americanos* (pp. 267–288). CLACSO.

Harvey, D. (2005). *Spaces of neoliberalization: towards a theory of uneven geographical development* (Vol. 8). Franz Steiner Verlag.

Lopez Sandoval, M., Robertsdotter, A., and Paredes, M. (2017). Space, Power, and Locality: The Contemporary Use of Territorio in Latin American Geography, *Journal of Latin American Geography*, 16(1), 43–67.

Maldonado-Torres, N. (2018). Analítica da colonialidade e da decolonialidade: algumas dimensões básicas. En: J. Bernardino-Costa, N. Maldonado-Torres, and R. Grosfoguel (Org.), *Decolonialidade e pensamento afrodiaspórico*, pp. 27–53. Autêntica Editora.

Motoki, C. (2018). O levante das comunidades tradicionais. Retrieved from http://reporterbrasil.org.br/comunidadestradicionais/o-levante-das-comunidades-tradicionais

Peet, R., and Hartwick, E. (2009). *Theories of development: Contentions, arguments, alternatives*. Guilford Publications.

Perreault, T., and Martin, P. (2005). Geographies of neoliberalism in Latin America, *Environment and Planning A*, 37(2), 191–201.

Saquet, M. (2007). *Abordagens e concepções de território*. São Paulo: Expressão Popular.
Saquet, M. (2018). A descoberta do território e outras premissas do desenvolvimento territorial, *Revista Brasileira de Estudos Urbanos e Regionais*, 20, 479–505.
Saquet, M., and Chicoski, P. (2022). Territorios Y (Des)Arrollo Raíz: contribuciones para una perspectiva de investigación y cooperación popular, decolonial y contra-hegemónica. En: D. Morales, L. Sariego, and T. Teixeira (Eds.), *Territorios y desarrollo: Teorías, debates y casos desde América Latina*. CICAP, Universidad de Costa Rica.
Schneider, S. (2010). Análisis multidimensional y escalar del desarrollo territorial en Brasil, *Eutopía: Revista de Desarrollo Económico Territorial*, (1), 25–49.
Stiglitz, J.E. (2002). *Globalization and Its Discontents*. New York: Norton.
Svampa, M. (2015). Commodities consensus: Neoextractivism and enclosure of the commons in Latin America, *South Atlantic Quarterly*, 114(1), 65–82.
Svampa, M. (2019). *Neo-extractivism in Latin America: socio-environmental conflicts, the territorial turn, and new political narratives*. Cambridge University Press.
Williamson, J. (1990). *Latin American adjustment: How much has happened?* (Vol. 4). Washington, DC: Institute for International Economics.
Willis, K. (2011). *Theories and Practices of Development*. Routledge.

Index

Pages in *italics* refer to figures, pages in **bold** refer to tables, and pages followed by "n" refer to notes.

For Product Safety Concerns and Information please contact our EU
representative GPSR@taylorandfrancis.com
Taylor & Francis Verlag GmbH, Kaufingerstraße 24, 80331 München, Germany

www.ingramcontent.com/pod-product-compliance
Ingram Content Group UK Ltd.
Pitfield, Milton Keynes, MK11 3LW, UK
UKHW021029021026
476168UK00012BA/1339
9781032650227